Focus On Jesus

Cycle C Sermons for Advent, Christmas, and Epiphany Based on the Gospel Texts

Derl Keefer

CSS Publishing Company, Inc.
Lima, Ohio

FOCUS ON JESUS
CYCLE C SERMONS FOR ADVENT, CHRISTMAS, AND EPIPHANY
BASED ON THE GOSPEL TEXTS

FIRST EDITION
Copyright © 2018
by CSS Publishing Co., Inc.

Published by CSS Publishing Company, Inc., Lima, Ohio 45807. All rights reserved. No part of this publication may be reproduced in any manner whatsoever without the prior permission of the publisher, except in the case of brief quotations embodied in critical articles and reviews. Inquiries should be addressed to: CSS Publishing Company, Inc., Permissions Department, 5450 N. Dixie Highway, Lima, Ohio 45807.

Library of Congress Cataloging-in-Publication Data
Names: Keefer, Derl G., 1949- author.
Title: Focus on Jesus : Cycle C sermons for Advent, Christmas, and Epiphany based on the Gospel texts / Derl Keefer.
Description: FIRST EDITION. | Lima : CSS Publishing Company, Inc., 2018.
Identifiers: LCCN 2018017139 | ISBN 9780788029240 (pbk.) | ISBN 078802924X (pbk.)
Subjects: LCSH: Bible. Gospels--Sermons. | Advent sermons. | Christmas sermons. | Epiphany--Sermons. | Church year sermons. | Common lectionary (1992). Year C.
Classification: LCC BS2555.54 K44 2018 | DDC 252/.6--dc23
LC record available at https://lccn.loc.gov/2018017139

For more information about CSS Publishing Company resources, visit our website at www.csspub.com, email us at csr@csspub.com, or call (800) 241-4056.

e-book:
ISBN-13: 978-0-7880-2925-7
ISBN-10: 0-7880-2925-8

ISBN-13: 978-0-7880-2924-0
ISBN-10: 0-7880-2924-X   PRINTED IN USA

Contents

Advent 1   5
Luke 2:23-56
Why Did Jesus Come?

Advent 2   13
Luke 3:1-6
A Commitment To Hope

Advent 3   21
Luke 3:7-18
A Commitment To Righteousness

Advent 4   29
Luke 1:39-45 (46-54)
The Song Of Servanthood

Nativity of OurLord   37
Luke 2:1-14 (15-20)
It's All About The Messiah

First Sunday After Christmas Day   45
Luke 2:41-51
Don't Miss Jesus

The Epiphany of Our Lord   53
Matthew 2:1-12
Walking In The Light

The Baptism of Our Lord   61
Luke 3:15-17, 21-22
The Baptism Of The Lord

Epiphany 2   69
John 2:1-11
Jesus Meets Our Needs

Epiphany 3   75
Luke 4:14-21
Jesus In Ministry — Us In Ministry

Epiphany 4   83
Luke 4:21-30
Rejecting The Message — Rejecting The Person

Epiphany 5   91
Luke 5:1-11
Christ's Call To Discipleship

Epiphany 6   97
Luke 6:17-26
Rules For Basic Living

Epiphany 7   103
Luke 6:27-36
Revolutionary Rules For Living

Transfiguration Sunday   109
Luke 9:28-36 (37-43a)
Rock Stars At The Top

Advent 1
Luke 2:23-56

Why Did Jesus Come?

My parents did not attend church when I was a child. A godly aunt and uncle asked my parents if I could attend church with them in 1951 when I was four. Fast forward to Christmas 2018 and I could probably count on one hand the number of times I have missed church. I entered pastoral ministry in 1970 while in seminary and have preached dozens of Christmas sermons. Each time I preach an Advent message I have to ask myself the same question, "Why did Jesus come to earth?" The ending story of our text tells of the paranoid parents finding Jesus in the temple sitting with the Bible scholars. You can almost hear the fear and frustration dripping from Mary's question to the young adolescent Jesus, "Son, why have you treated us like this? Your father and I have been anxiously searching for you" (Luke 2:48).

Jesus used a tactic that he would use effectively throughout his ministry. He responded with a question of his own. "Did you not know that I must be about my Father's business?" (Luke 2:49b).

Why did Jesus come to planet earth? Throughout the scriptural text we will ask that question often. It will become evident why Jesus came, *Selon la volonte de Dieu*, "according to God's will."

Our story begins eight days after the birth of Jesus. All the glamour and spectacular events had faded into normal life. The new parents were fulfilling the ritual activities of their religion. They took their son to the temple in Jerusalem to offer a sacrifice. Bruce Larson noted, "Mary and Joseph were proceeding with all the usual Jewish customs in connection with this most unusual infant." (Communicator's Commentary, Luke, page 55).

Two unique and godly people were in the temple worshiping, praising, reflecting, praying, watching, and anticipating to hear from God. On this day their long expectant wait was over. Separately, these two would receive a message from God about the baby they saw with their own eyes…God's answer to their longing!

Simeon and Anna would come upon them and both would recognize the importance of this child for the future of all people…Jews and Gentiles. We know very little about Simeon or Anna.

Simeon, according to Luke's gospel, was just, devout, waiting in prayerful expectancy of help for Israel's spiritual good. One other important note, "and the Holy Spirit was on him" (Luke 2:25 Message Bible). He was a servant of God waiting for instruction and refused to leave his post until it happened!

Simeon was overwhelmed by the power of the Holy Spirit and he swooped the baby Jesus up into his arms then gave a prayer of thanksgiving to God for the child. In that moment of thanksgiving his search for the promised messiah had ended. He had now seen for himself the light of the world. Simeon prophesied that Mary's heart would break because her son would be rejected. But the rejection would cause humanity to see with honest eyes what he had come to do!

The other character in our text is Anna and she is called a prophetess. She broke into an anthem of praise to God and talked about the freedom that would come to Jerusalem because of the child Jesus.

Why did Jesus come?

I. Jesus came to be the fulfillment of prophecy (Luke 2:26a).

The prophets were individuals called by God to reveal his purpose, will and/or action on the world's history map. Their proclamation included the holy and divine word of God through either judgment or grace. John Walvoord wrote, "The fundamental purpose of prophecy is to give believers the necessary facts to plan wisely for future events that will eventually take place."

The commissioned prophet declared apocalyptic events and prediction of the future, but never forgot that it was in the light of "word of the Lord" and was relevant to their present situation. Prophecy could take place in the immediate future or hundreds of years if not more later.

Wilfred Winget declared that the New Testament writers saw in the whole pattern of Old Testament history, as well as specific statements, God's promise of the preparation for God's climatic saving revelation in Jesus as the Christ revealed in his life, death, and resurrection.

Both Simeon and Anna were probably students of the prophets and anticipated the one who would come to deliver Israel out of its moral fog. I do not believe they were concerned with their peers' concept of a warrior king opposing Roman domination, but rather the one who would oppose Satan, hell, evil and sin... the spiritual warrior king.

These two saints of God were prophets in their own rights as we will understand later on.

II.   Jesus came to be the Messiah (Luke 2:26b).

The word "Messiah" is derived from the Hebrew word *meshiach* and means "anointed" or "the anointed." The Greek term for "Messiah" is "Christos" and to us in English it is "Christ." John Riley, (Beacon Dictionary of Theology, page 335), wrote that "On the early pages of the New Testament, 'Christos' occurs with the definite article, 'the Christ' "(as in Matthew 1616; Matthew 27:22; John 4;29; I John 2:22 and I John 5:1). These writers wanted us to know beyond a shadow of a doubt that Jesus was the "anointed one"…the only one who comes directly from heaven and God's heartbeat.

Over the decades and centuries following the destruction and desecration of Judea in 586 BC, the populace of the Jews found their hopes and dreams centering upon an earthly Messiah who would restore them to independence. They desire the reestablishment of the monarch by a descendant of David. As you read the Old Testament prophets, Haggai and Zechariah, the future king would be the Messiah God.

God's vision of his Messiah was different. His desire was to have a moral and spiritual Messiah. He would be the one who would punish sin, usher in righteousness, and bring peace over the hearts and lives of all people. The spiritual and earthly Jerusalem would be the epicenter of universal joy.

"The true and the living God saw his Messiah as the servant of humanity. His mission would be to spread the knowledge of the true God to the ends of the earth…not by imposing his will on others, but by uncomplaining endurance of contempt, injustice, suffering and death" (F.F. Bruce, New Testament History, p. 128). Who is this Messiah you may ask? It is the anointed Lord as the angels proclaimed to the lowly shepherds in Bethlehem! (Luke 2:11).

So what does that mean for us at Christmas time, 2018? Everything! This Messiah has come to be your God! Now. Today. He is God's heartbeat who desires to live in you to bring your life together.

During World War II a bomb fell near Reims Cathedral and shattered their beautiful stain glass window into thousands of pieces. The entire village searched the area until all the pieces could be salvaged. After the war was over, skilled artisans put the window back to its original beauty as each separate piece was leaded into the perfect whole.

Frank Court commented about that window and its application to life when he said that "religion enables us to pick up life's fragments and re-dream our dreams, relive our hopes, rethink our faith, until the light of God once again shines through the window of our life."

That is why Jesus came…to be your personal Messiah!

III. Jesus came to bring salvation to our world (Luke 2:30-35).

When God first developed our world it was a "very good" world that Adam and Eve inherited. He made things with beauty, symmetry, and habitable for all. No sin darkened the horizon. In Genesis 3 everything changed with the temptation story and the ultimate weakening and then the fall from grace. This evil was the result of our parents' disobedience to the known command of God. So that we are clear on the matter of sin, although God is the creator and sovereign ruler of all things in life, he is not the author of our sinfulness. When our parents doubted the word of God forbidding them to pick the fruit of the tree of righteousness — their purity collapsed. With that came the fear and dread of meeting God! It still occurs. Sin is current in our lives today. The problem of sin is that it is universal for the Gentiles (non-Jews) according to Luke 2:31-32a and for the Jews (Luke 2:32b).

We need a remedy that takes away our sin in order that we might be righteous before the holy God. We are powerless to save ourselves through good works or attempts to keep the Ten Commandments or the Mosaic Law. Honestly, the law only exposes our sin and our desperate need for salvation.

As Christians we firmly believe that salvation is offered through Jesus. Several years ago I saw a picture of the nativity scene. The manger showed the baby Jesus laying in the straw, but with the shadow of the cross over the crib.

Christmas and Easter are so intertwined as Jesus came as a baby to this earth with one goal…to die for our sins. His life and death would bring about a change in our destiny.

- Christ's sinless life would become our substitute for our guilty sinfulness.
- Christ's death involves the removal of our personal guilt.
- Christ's death would commute our sentences of spiritual death.
- Christ's death would allow us to be adopted into the family of God.

- Christ's death signals that once we have believed in Christ as our sacrifice for sin we can immediately experience new life in him.
- Christ's death is an ongoing process as our relationship continues in him.
- Christ's death is an eternal life with God. We have truly come to the at-one-ment with God through Christ!

Charles Swindoll told the story of a bazaar held in a village in India. People brought their wares to be sold and traded. One farmer brought a whole covey of quail. He had tied a string around one leg of each of the birds. The other end of the strings were tied around a ring which fit loosely over a central stick. He had taught the quail to walk in a circle. No one at the open air bazaar seemed interested. Toward the end of the day a devout Brahman came along who believed in the Hindu idea of respect for all life. He bought all of them. Then to the surprise of the farmer the Brahman said, "Let them go…set them free."

With the shrug of the shoulder the farmer bent down and snipped the strings off the quail. They were free! What happened next was interesting. Instead of flying off into the sunset those birds simply continued marching around and around in a circle. Finally, the Brahman and the farmer chased them off into the air, but a little way down the road they landed and resumed their predictable march. Free, unfettered, released, yet they kept going in circles as if still tied together.

Swindoll's last sentence was a warning to all of us. "Salvation cuts the strings of sin. It's time to stop marching and start flying." God through Christ has set us free to live…so live!

IV. Jesus came to answer the world's question about God (Luke 2:47-50).

Going from the scene of the presentation of the baby Jesus at the temple to the young Jesus again at the temple, we begin to see the development of the reason Jesus came. When questioned by his mother about why he had stayed in Jerusalem as they had pushed homeward he gives the answer: "Didn't you know that I had to be about my Father's business?" (Luke 2:49).

What was the business that Jesus was discussing? He was listening to the teachers of Israel (the professors of the law) and asking pertinent questions. He was drawing them into conversation. The Bible says, "Everyone who heard him was amazed at his understanding and his answers" (Luke 2:47).

Christ's business is to help you understand God. We can see the Father's love, care, compassion, and heart through Christ. His entrance into the world put flesh on God.

A little boy said that Jesus is the best photograph of God.

Conclusion

Today, Christ wants to help you know God in all of his fullness! Your salvation, hope, and understanding is in the Christ who has come to give *you* life!

Amen.

Advent 2
Luke 3:1-6

A Commitment To Hope

The story is told of young boy in a church Christmas program who had one line to remember. His role was that of the Angel of the Lord and his one line consisted of: "Behold, I bring you good tidings."

He wasn't clear about the word "tidings" so he asked his mother what it meant. She defined it as "news."

Sunday morning the play was going smoothly and all was well. He was sent onto the stage as the Angel of the Lord announcing to the shepherds about God's message. When he got on stage and looked out at the crowd he froze! Stage fright overcame him and his brain went to mush. He couldn't remember the line for anything. Then all of a sudden his mom's definition flashed back and he blurted out to the shepherds, "Hey! Boys, have I got news for you!"

John, the cousin of Jesus, is the man God had chosen to be the instrument that would lay the foundation for the ministry of Jesus. God called John to preach and his message sounded like the prophets of Old Testament times. John preached that the people had to repent of their sins and change their lifestyle from complacency and carnality to hope and holiness in the God of Israel. He was laying the foundation for the one who would come after him who could actually forgive their sins and bring purity to their lives.

I.   **Making preparation for hope (Luke 3:4a).**

The preparation that John made was an announcement of good news! The one that the people of Israel had long been waiting for was in their very presence. The long awaited Messiah stirred among them.

The message of hope is that "all flesh will see the salvation of God" (Luke 3:6 NKJV). John's message comes approximately 30 years after the shepherds on the hillsides around Nazareth heard basically the same message. The angel said, "…behold, I bring you good tidings of great joy which shall be to all people. For there is born to you this day in the city of David a Savior." (Luke 2:10-11a). What does a Savior do for his people? He saves them from their predicament.

John's role at that Advent season was about preparation. His message to people in 2018 is the same. We need to prepare our hearts and homes for the Christ who has come to save us. This is a celebration of the birth of the Savior. He is saying to us, "Get ready." Make preparation for the night we celebrate as the entrance of the Savior into the world. Think, pray, meditate, and put your actions where your heart is now! God has sent the Savior to change your world.

We are making preparation for the hope of salvation that comes through Christ. Someone once wrote that John's bold and brazen call for repentance is not something we can do on our own — no matter what we do or say, or how much we try we fall short to produce our own salvation. As many good deeds as we do, we still cannot succeed.

The hope of salvation is the work that God has provided in the way we humans are to be delivered from our sinful condition, by the sacrificial death of Jesus on the cross and the authorization through the resurrection. Death on the cross would only be a martyr's death if it were not for the power of the resurrection. Jesus entrance into the world marks the beginning of our rescue…our salvation deliverance. John is preparing the way for our grasp of that glorious truth.

II. Making Preparation for the good news (Luke 3:4b).

I read about a 12 year old boy named Jim who wrote a note to God. It said, "Dear God, was there anything special about Bethlehem or did you just figure that it would be as good a place as any to start a franchise?"

The world has trouble with the good news scenario because it started with a baby in a humble setting. The Jewish people wanted a warrior king who would emancipate them from foreign rule and bring back the Davidic dynasty of power and authority.

The Good News is the incarnation of Jesus combining God and humanity as one. That is difficult for us to wrap our minds and hearts around, but as a matter of fact and faith it is true. The incarnation is the living embodiment of the invisible God seen through the human Jesus. He is the Messiah and is the very expression of God come to earth to bring God's love, salvation, and hope to a world lost in its own sinful ways.

The Good News is God has come to identify with us. Billy Strayhorn wrote about a girl by the name of Alice who lived in an orphanage. She was called to the office once again to be "interviewed" for a possible placement in a home seeking to adopt a child. Her hope wasn't very high, because it happened all too often. She would hear voices on the other side of the door and they would use words like "slow" or "difficult" to describe her.

Each time she would be asked in the office and there would be an inch by inch scrutiny. She felt like a specimen under a microscope or a slab of meat hanging in a butcher shop, not the homeless, parentless little girl that was her. Interviews brought back memories of the times she was ignored after the woman saw how poorly her dress fit. There was also the time she was laughed at because of her stuttering. Worst of all were the times she was rejected because they said her clubfoot would make her too clumsy.

Now she was being "examined" again. This time it was by a young man and woman sitting in front of her gazing directly at her. All of those bad memories came racing back into her heart and mind. She felt so very self-conscious and attempted to hide her misshapen foot behind the good one.

As Alice looked at the young couple she thought the woman was beautiful. Her hair was soft and shined. Her face was clean and bright. Her dress was immaculately pressed. Everything about her cried out perfection. The man got up slowly and walked around Alice. At times he would stop, glance toward his wife, and raise an eyebrow. After what seemed an eternity to Alice, he sat down next to his wife. They looked into one another's eyes for a long time, not speaking. Then he turned to the superintendent of the orphanage and said, "Yes, she's the one."

Alice was stunned. In a stuttering voice she said, "You mean you want me to be your serving girl?"

The young wife smiled and said, "Oh, no Alice. We mean we want you to be our daughter."

Alice couldn't believe it. No one had ever said they wanted her! She had dreamed of it, but she could hardly believe it. She asked, "You mean you really want me to be your daughter…to live in your house?"

The man spoke up, "Yes. We can't have children of our own. We have so much love to give, and we want to give it to you. We want you to be happy."

Recalling all of the times she had been rejected, she had to ask, "But why me?"

With that the woman smiled and then slowly reached down and pulled her floor length dress up enough to reveal her own malformed foot. Then with reassurance and understanding she said to Alice, "Today, we want you to be our child. Please, Alice, let us love you."

That is just like God. In Jesus He has come to identify with our pain, hurts, struggles and failures. He knows the joys of life as well as the temptations. In the Bethlehem stable he came, not just looking like one of us, but truly as one of us. He has come to be our Savior and will leave no one out who will accept him into their lives!

III. Making preparation for salvation (Luke 3:6).

Luke quoted the prophet Isaiah to remind us that everyone will see the salvation of God. Who is the salvation of God? Jesus is his name!

His salvation can be grasped both as an intellectual pursuit as well as a spiritual endeavor. We are encouraged to use logic and our mind to ask good questions about our spiritual and religious life. Asking good questions challenges us to think through what we believe, helping us on our spiritual quest as we follow God on this journey of salvation for a lifetime.

His salvation of an individual's soul is of utmost importance. C.S. Lewis wrote that this individual soul is "…more important than the production of all the epics and tragedies in the world." This vital importance is summed up in John 3:16, "For God so loved the world that he gave his one and only Son, that whoever believes in him shall not perish but have eternal life." The reason for the season? God gave his Son.

His salvation lights up my world. His light dispels the sin of legalism, the rejection of antinomianism, the insatiable vices of morality, hatred, racism, injustice, and the fear of Satan, evil and hell! No longer do I have to live in darkness.

Every person in the world can come to Jesus. He is the shining light for all of us. Philip Bliss wrote about this in 1875 in his hymn "The Light of the World is Jesus."*(In the public domain.)*

> *The whole world was lost in the darkness of sin;*
> *The light of the world is Jesus.*
> *Like sunshine at noonday his glory shone in;*
> *The light of the world is Jesus.*
> *REFRAIN:*
> *Come to the light; 'tis shining for thee,*
> *Sweetly the light has dawned upon me.*
> *Once I was blind, but now I can see.*
> *The light of the world is Jesus.*

Conclusion

Decades ago near the North Pole, with the night lasting for months, when the people expected that day was about to dawn, some messengers got up to the highest point to watch. When they saw the first streaks of the dawning of the day they put on their brightest possible clothing, and embraced each other and cried, "Behold the sun! and the cry went around all the land, "Behold the sun."

John looked forward to the new dawn of life. The cry from John and the cry from heaven on that Christmas night was "Behold the S-O-N!" and the son of righteousness has come. Salvation has come to all who will receive him.

Amen.

Advent 3
Luke 3:7-18

A Commitment To Righteousness

Moline, Illinois, September, 1977 was the place and date for a special gift that Terry Schafer purchased for her policeman husband, David. It was a pre-Christmas gift. She had a fear that it might be too expensive, but nothing was too good for her husband! She loved him with all of her heart and wanted this to be special.

Slipping into one of the stores that was on her list she found the exact item she wanted, but it was too expensive for her to buy outright. She talked with the salesman and told him that her husband was a police officer in their town. After a bit they negotiated a payment deal that Terry could afford. She gave him the first payment and he suggested that the store wrap it up and she could take it home. She was elated!

Author Charles Swindoll wrote, "And like a lot of us, she wasn't able to keep the secret. So that night as David unwrapped the gift, Terry stood there beaming. He was thrilled at her thoughtfulness and covered her with hugs and kisses."

Moline, Illinois, Oct 1, 1977. Patrolman David Schafer was working the evening shift when he received a call on his police radio. There was a robbery in progress at a local drugstore. Rushing to the scene he arrived just as the suspect was speeding off. Patrolman

Schafer sped in hot pursuit of the perpetrator, but three blocks from the robbery the suspect suddenly stopped on the side of the road.

Seated behind the wheel the robber didn't move. David cautiously approached the suspect when about three feet from the driver's door it flew open and the driver took out a .45-caliber automatic pistol and fired a slug that went right to David's stomach.

At seven o'clock the following morning, David's wife, Terry answered the door after a knock. A policeman stood in front of her and shared that during a robbery her husband had been shot. Calmly the officer explained that David was badly bruised, but alive.

Terry Schafer mulled over in her mind that she was so happy that her Christmas present was given early. If she had waited to December 25, 1977, her husband would have been dead.

Christmas had come early that year because David had with him the gift of life his wife could not wait to give: his brand-new bulletproof vest.

Swindoll commented, "And that's why Christ came, to give us a vest of righteousness, to pay the price with his blood, that he might protect us with the shield that sin could never penetrate."

*Charles Swindoll, *The Tale of the Tardy Oxcart* (Nashville: Word Publishing, 1998, pp. 496-497).

Each believer is instructed to hunger and thirst for righteousness by Jesus himself. Righteousness is transformed into right living through the word of God and the power of the Holy Spirit.

I.   Repentance: a part of righteousness (Luke 3:8).

The people of John's day were in need of what he was preaching...repentance and living right. John knew their sins for they were obvious. Their need for God was also obvious and the prophet was there to point them to the remedy.

John's message didn't die when he did. His message spans the timeline to today. Our world is still in need of turning from sin and receiving the gift of salvation.

John's message was that Jesus was coming to cancel their spiritual debts and remove their sin obligations from the book of justice. Sin, placed on Jesus, would never be held against anyone who accepts Christ into their life. Why? It is because Jesus Christ died for us and paid the cost for our salvation.

The story is told of a young man who entered a bank in New York City attempting to get a loan from one of the bank officers. After completing all of the paperwork he was a bit surprised that it was taking so long for a reply. He anxiously observed that the loan officer kept going back and forth to his manager's desk.

Finally the paperwork was completed. He was startled when he turned to leave because he was met with the flashes of cameras going off in his face and people began to crowd around him. It struck him that he must have done something wrong and the fear was written on his face.

Quickly he was relieved to discover that instead of being in the wrong place at the wrong time, he was in the right place at the right time. The manager of the bank handed his loan papers back to him and told him that he would not have to repay the loan! He was fortunate enough to have borrowed the money that included the one billionth dollar that the lending institution had ever loaned out. In honor of that fact, his debt would never be recorded in the books.

John the Baptist preached to the people around the Jordan and beyond that a redeemer was coming to cancel their debt of sin. The Messiah was coming to take their debts and remove their sin obligation from the books. At Christmas we rejoice in the knowledge that the Messiah is Jesus who entered this world to pay the price for our sin. The shadow of the cross always lies across the manger scene.

II.   Conviction: A part of righteousness (Luke 3:10).

The message John preached penetrated the hearts and minds of his listeners. Conviction began to seep into their very souls as the light began to dawn on them.

Conviction comes from the Holy Spirit as part of his "job description." It produces within humanity a sense of guilt and condemnation of sin. As the Holy Spirit convicts; our role is to act upon it and allow God to change sinful actions and attitudes to thoughts and acts of righteousness.

Tony Compolo recalled a deeply moving incident that happened in a Christian junior high camp where he served. One of the junior high boys was afflicted with spastic paralysis that affected his speech. Each time he would talk it was in a halting voice. The kids would heartlessly ridicule him. When he asked a question of someone that person would answer haltingly and mimicking his speech. One night the cabin group chose him to lead the devotions before the entire camp. It was just another effort to poke some "fun" at his expense. The time arrived and the disabled young man unashamedly stood up, and in his strained, slurred manner…each word coming with enormous effort… he simply said, "Jesus loves me — and I love Jesus!"

Conviction rolled over that junior high camp as God began to speak to their hearts about how they had treated one of his children. Many began to cry. Most of them repented and apologized to the young man. Revival gripped the camp. Campolo said that years later that he met men in the ministry who came to Christ because of the courage of that handicapped teenager who was brave enough to share his love for Jesus!

I believe that God convicts individuals of their sins to change their lives, but I also believe that God convicts Christians to be more compassionate, honest people, peace makers, justice seekers, integrity lovers, morally upright, and much more.

When is the last time God convicted you? How did you respond?

III. Responding: a part of righteousness (Luke 3:15-18).

Listening to John's message and feeling the conviction of the Holy Spirit — the people had a choice. They could either walk away and do nothing about it or, they could respond and act on the message. Many in the crowd left, but many responded to his call for change.

Acting on faith in Jesus is required before salvation becomes reality and change is initiated into our life style.

Responding includes *reconciliation*. Humanity has been alienated from God because of sin. Paul spoke to that in Romans 5:6-11 in where he called unsaved people as "powerless," "ungodly," "sinners," and "God's enemies." The remedy is the removal of the enmity that stands between God and humanity. What is the remedy? Paul put it into perspective as he wrote

"When we were God's enemies, we were reconciled to him through the death of his Son" (Romans 5:10). He wrote to the Colossian church, "He has reconciled you by Christ's physical body through death to present you holy in his sight, without blemish and free from accusation" (Colossians 1:22).

Responding includes obedience. The bottom line for all believers is that obedience is never an option. Wendell Johnson observed that the predominant Hebrew word for obedience is *sama* and the New Testament words are *akouo* and *hyakouo* which means, "to hear intelligently and attentively and respond appropriately."

Christians demonstrate to others that we belong to Christ when we believe in him, obey his word, and by loving others along with doing his holy will.

Responding includes worship. In the New Testament and throughout the history of the church we state, "Jesus is Lord." Because he is Lord, and sovereign, he is to be worshiped (Luke 4:4-8). As such:

- The focal preaching of the apostles was the Lordship of Jesus. It should be the focal point of today's church. We must focus on Jesus.
- The central subject of the church is the leadership of Jesus. The church's actions are under the direct order of the Lord's leadership to fulfill his directives to be compassionate, caring, socially concerned, but most of all, spiritually oriented leading people to a saving relationship.
- The people of God have been justified by God's grace and specifically incorporate the reckoning of the righteousness of Christ to the believer. It

is pure faith in him. The other world religions base justification on human effort. Is it any wonder that we worship and praise the living God?

Conclusion

"As a Christian, transform your righteous standing before God into righteous living for God through the Word of God and the power of the Holy Spirit." (Quoted from "The Theological Wordbook", Word Publishing, 2000).

Amen.

Advent 4
Luke 1:39-45 (46-54)

The Song Of Servanthood

Weddings are beautiful and exciting events with an abundance of anticipation. There is so much to do. The "who, what, where, how and why" questions all need to be answered. The bride's dress needs to be just perfect for her. The bridesmaids' dresses are to be considered and ordered. Flowers need to be ordered from the florist. The guest list must be made and invitations sent. Registration for gifts at different stores should be processed. Oh, and don't forget the groom and his entourage must be given their lists! A flurry of excitement abounds!

One wonders if that was going through the mind of young Mary of Nazareth (Luke 1:26-27). Her pledge of marriage to Joseph was a commitment of love, faith, and loyalty to her future husband. Everything had to be "just perfect" when the time came for the wedding. Her desire was for nothing less.

On one fateful night her world turned topsy-turvy. Everything changed! According to the scriptures (Luke 1:26-38) an angel appeared to Mary with an announcement from God. She had been selected as the entrusted woman to give birth to the Messiah of Israel…and the whole world. Flashing through Mary's mind was this incredible and sobering news. Obviously it would occur after she was married to Joseph. As the angel kept speaking, her mind began to comprehend that Gabriel was not talking about after she was married, but that she was going to become pregnant before the wedding! Luke states that Mary was greatly troubled at his words and unsure of what he meant. Being a faithful and spiritual Jewish woman, she wasn't sure how this would happen. Catch her confusion as Luke recorded the conversation, "How will this be since I am a virgin?" (Luke 1:34).

Gabriel gave her the specifics, "The Holy Spirit will come on you, and the power of the most high will overshadow you. So the holy one to be born will be called the Son of God…for no word from God will ever fail" (Luke 1:35-36 NIV).

Her response should be the response of every faithful follower of God. "I am the Lord's servant…May your word to me be fulfilled" (Luke 1:38 NIV).

After the Holy Spirit impregnated Mary, she realized that this would not be understood by her parents or Joseph. As time passed Mary asked to go visit her relative and friend, Elizabeth who lived in a town in the hill country of Judea far enough away from Nazareth where there would be no questions. Mary desperately needed someone to confide, in get wise counseling and someone to share her secret with whom she could trust.

As Mary knocked on the door and was let in by Elizabeth, the baby inside of Elizabeth kicked and made her feel good about all that was happening. According to scripture it wasn't just a good feeling, but a confirmation as she was filled with the Holy Spirit. She exclaimed in a loud voice of excitement, "Blessed are you among women, and blessed is the child you will bear...Blessed is she who has believed that the Lord would fulfill his promises to her!"(Luke 1:40-45 NIV).

The word, "blessed," describes happiness to those whom God favors or smiles upon. At that moment Elizabeth encouraged Mary's faith, and after this spontaneous blessing Mary began a song of praise and servanthood. Theologians call this song the "Magnificant" and it is dedicated to the adoration of Mary's closest friend and ally, Jehovah God, himself.

Today we want to look closely at Mary's song and what it meant to her and to us.

I. As God's servant, Mary's song is one of happiness (Luke 1:39-45).

Actor-comedian Dom DeLuise, whose affable nature made him a popular actor for decades with movie and television audiences as well as directors and fellow actors, tells that there was a dark time in his life when little made him smile. He stated that everything was wrong and it seemed that life was hopeless and that he was feeling useless. As Christmas was approaching, Deluise's son asked what his dad wanted as a Christmas present. DeLuise reluctantly replied, "Happiness...and you can't give it to me." Christmas day came and as the family opened their gifts, the boy handed his dad a piece of cardboard with one word scribbled on it...HAPPINESS. The son said, "See pop, I can give you happiness!' DeLuise laughed and he said in that moment his depression was shattered.

What brings you happiness in life? Joseph Addison said that the grand essentials to happiness in this life are something to do, someone to love, and something to hope for.

Mary had a commission from God to bring life to

the Messiah. It would take her to the depths of despair and the ecstasy of joy. She would watch her son die on a cross probably — the hardest experience for any mother to witness. She would also encounter his resurrection. She would live the rest of her life fulfilling God's will. As Christians we are to live our lives doing the will of God.

Mary loved Jesus and was filled with love for others. She was among the people in the upper room who were baptized with the Holy Spirit on the day of Pentecost and shared God's love with those in Jerusalem. (Acts 1:14). Her desire was to communicate her son's message to a world so desperately in need of him. As Christians we are called to evangelize the world and tell them of God's love according to the great commission (Matthew 28:16-18).

Mary had a deep abiding happiness in God. Do we?

II. As God's servant, Mary's song is one of glorifying God (Luke 1:46-51).

The Bible infers that God had first place in Mary's life. The song of glory came from deep within her soul and spirit and rose to her lips as she gave glory to the redeemer of life!

Giving God glory is far more than a sentimental expression of feeling. It is the absolute knowledge that we glorify God for his redemptive act in our lives.

God's redemptive process comes through the whole Christ event.

First, it was from the beginning that this plan of salvation originated. John wrote in his first epistle (letter), "That which was from the beginning, which we have heard, which we have seen with our eyes, which we have looked at and our hands have touched — this we proclaim concerning the Word of life. The life appeared; we have seen it and testify to it, and we proclaim to you the eternal life, which was with the Father and has appeared to us...And our fellowship is with the Father and with his Son, Jesus Christ" (1 John 1:1-3 NIV).

Second, it was through the birth that this plan continued. We read it in Luke's account when the angel appeared to Mary and said, "The Holy Spirit will come on you, and the power of the Most High will overshadow you. So the holy one to be born will be called the Son of God" (Luke 1:35).

Third, it was through faith in Jesus that the plan unfolds. Jesus, talking with Nicodemus said, "For God so loved the world that he gave his one and only Son, that whoever believes in him shall not perish but have eternal life. For God did not send his Son into the world to condemn the world, but to save the world through him" (John 3:16-17 NIV).

Fourth, God's plan culminated at Calvary and the cross of Jesus. By shedding his blood on the cross, Jesus took our punishment that we rightly deserved because of our sinfulness, and offered us his righteousness. We essentially make a trade by faith; we give him our sin and its accompanying death penalty and he gives us his righteousness and abiding presence.

Peter taught it correctly when he wrote, "He himself bore our sins in his body on the cross, so that we might die to sins and live for righteousness..." (1 Peter 2:24 NIV).

Fifth, the plan's ultimate victory came through God's resurrection of Jesus. Without the resurrection Jesus would only be a martyr, but because of the resurrection he is our Savior!

Luke's writing says that the women who followed Jesus went to the tomb. When they arrived angels were waiting and asked, "Why do you look for the living among the dead? He is not here; he has risen! Remember how he told you while he was still with you in Galilee: 'The Son of Man must be delivered over to the hands of sinners, be crucified and on the third day be raised again.'" (Luke 24:6-7 NIV).

"The resurrection is God's 'Amen!' to Christ's statement, 'It is finished'" (Lewis Johnson).

Mary's servant song of glorifying God — the song all of us should be singing during this Christmas season!

III. As God's servant, Mary's song is one of faith (Luke 1:54-56).

Her song reflects the heritage that builds on faith. Someone wrote, "Some generations are more aware of what they have achieved than of what they have inherited, forgetting that the heritage makes the achievement possible."

As a child I attended a small church where a group of "ordinary" Christians surrounded me with their love and encouragement. They helped instill within my heart a desire for faith. It culminated in my acceptance of Jesus and conversion to a Christ life walk as a lad of eight. Those "ordinary" saints gave me a heritage that still lives over six decades beyond. Family names that mean nothing to you, mean everything to me for they taught me the rudiments of faith and helped bring me to maturity. They stood shoulder to shoulder with me when I felt a "call" to ministry supporting me through prayer, concern, and encouragement in words. Every sermon I have preached, the pastoral work I engaged in, the denominational assignments given me, the various speaking engagements, along with the books and articles published over these past seventy years all reflect on their faith in me so many years ago.

Today, many people helped formulate your faith. Like Mary, think about those people and thank God for what they helped instill into your heart, life and work.

Conclusion:

Bruce Larson tells the story of being interviewed once by a reporter who had covered Mother Teresa's visit to Boys Town, USA. Larson asked him about that visit and her reaction to the famous town. The reporter said that the priest and administrators showed her all over the grounds including the dormitories, the classrooms, the gymnasium, the dining hall and more. At the end of the tour according to the reporter, Mother Teresa turned to the head priest and said, "You have all this, but do you really love them?" This is the ultimate virtue of servanthood. It is not about social programs, numbers of things we accomplish, funds that we raise, or achievements we produce. It is about the love of Christ that we instill into all of those projects. It comes through our happiness, glorifying God and faith in Christ.

Let us praise God together in whatever language we speak as his servants.

Alaba Dios, a quien todas bendiciones fluye;
Alaba El, todos las criaturas aqui abajo;
Alaba el encima, vosotros anfitriones divino;
Alaba El Padre, El Hijo, y El Espiritu Santo
Amen!   (Spanish)

Praise God, from who all blessings flow;
Praise him, all creatures here below;
Praise him above, ye heavenly host
Praise Father, Son, and Holy Ghost
Amen.

Nativity of Our Lord
Luke 2:1-14 (15-20)

It's All About The Messiah

I read an old legend about a Christmas party that Satan and his pack of demons were having in hell. As the demonic guests were departing, one laughed and grinned and sarcastically said to Satan, "Merry Christmas your majesty!" At that, Satan replied with a growl, "Yes, keep it merry. If they ever get serious about it, we'll all be in trouble."

Today the focus is all about the Messiah and we need to be serious about it. It is the birth of the baby Jesus, the Messiah. It is the coming of God…the doctrine of incarnation. It is the intervention of God's presence among humanity.

As someone observed — it was the year of destiny. According to Greek theology, the planet Jupiter entered the Great Conjunction by proclaiming the coming ruler of the final Golden Age. In Rome Augustus was at the apex of his career. On the Nile in Egypt the Emperor was being celebrated as the freedom-giving god, Jupiter. On the Euphrates the astrologers were setting out for Palestine to see the promised king of peace. The country of Israel was a different setting. There was a tempest brewing.

Stauffer related to his readers that Herod had been demoted several months before Quirinius' census-takers were spreading like a swarm of locusts descending upon all the towns and small villages of Israel, with swords in their hands. The bureaucracy ran rampant and the people fought back with resistance including rebel bands. Six thousand Pharisees refused to take the imperial oath to Jupiter that Rome demanded. Herod, the puppet king of Israel was nervous. He did all within his power to satisfy Rome's tax collectors and commissioners. There was sedition and plots whispered throughout the land. Herod's ears were everywhere and whenever he suspected that a plot to overthrow his government was bubbling up, he acted with vengeance. In Samaria he had the two Hasmonaean princes killed. Along with the princes he had three hundred officers faithful to the Hasmoneans assassinated. His eyes were on anyone who might be a descendent of David.

It is this apocalyptic environment that Jesus came into the world…the son of David born in the ancient, holy, royal city of Bethlehem.

I. Christmas is about the birth of the Messiah (Luke 2:1-7).

People in Western culture who have grown up in the church know the elementary elements of the story. Today the story is different. With the decline of Christianity and church attendance many have no idea of the events. Let me just recount some of the events.

Rome decided it would be a strategic decision to find out the population of their Roman states and satellite lands. The Gospel writer, Luke begins the Christmas story with the quick mention of Caesar Augustus, who was the biological nephew of Julius Caesar and Augustus, who became Julius' adoptive son. It was Augustus who led Rome's transformation from a republic form of government to an empire that would last for 200 years. Augustus shrewdly combined military might, institutional building projects and lawmaking tenants to lay the foundation for his rule. There would be no time in history where the birth of the Messiah could have been more appropriate up to that time.

Luke told us that Joseph and Mary went up from the town of Nazareth in Galilee to Judea to the sleepy village of Bethlehem because Joseph's heritage was from there. Old Testament prophet Micah wrote 700 years before the birth of Jesus that the Messiah would be born in Bethlehem (Micah 5:1-2). The meaning of Bethlehem is "house of bread." What an appropriate place for Jesus to be born. He said of himself, "I am the bread of life." (John 6:35a) and continued in that verse to say to people, "Whoever goes to me will never go hungry" (John 6:35b).

The gospel writer sketched in another character in his story...the innkeeper. This businessman has been painted as a villain by most of us. Probably more accurately he was busy and his inn was full. He had no idea who he was refusing a room to at that moment. Tell me what paying customer would he kick out? Wouldn't you be upset if he tried to take your room? He did the best that he could with the situation at hand. He was being expedient like most of us today. So don't be too hard on him. "In the season when we celebrate this birth we get so busy with Christmas cards and presents, with year-end internal revenue matters, with shopping and cooking, that there is no room in our lives for the most important guest of all. Like the innkeeper, we are not villains; we're just preoccupied and harried." (Bruce Larson, *The Communicator's Commentary — Luke*, p. 48).

Joseph and Mary took the stable offered by the innkeeper. It was there that Mary gave birth to her son Jesus. This little baby who fit so snuggly into his mother's arms, who felt so light in the rough hands of his stepfather, Joseph…this baby was the Messiah sent from God the Father to become the Messiah to Israel and the world. The etymology *Meshiac* means "anointed one." In the Old Testament when it was applied to persons, the term indicates induction into a sacred office. It was applied exceptionally to prophets, occasionally to the chief priests and most commonly to the king of Israel, who was called Messiah of Yahweh (1 Samuel 24:6, Ezekiel 29:7, Isaiah 54:1).

Once Judea was destroyed in 586 BC the Jews found their hopes centering upon an earthly establishment of the monarchy by a descendant of David. But the prophets began to help their people to understand that the Messiah was so much more than an earthly king.

This new Messiah would spread the knowledge of the true God to the very ends of the world. His plan was to do it by not imposing his will on others, but by uncomplaining endurance of contempt, injustice, suffering, and death. Who was this Messiah? It was the one who lays bare the kingdom of God and the realities of God's redemptive work. It was Christ who calls a wayward Israel and world back to a loving holy God. The baby Jesus who would grow into manhood and become God's Messiah for the world. He is also our Messiah and he comes directly from heaven for our salvation!

II.   Christmas is about the Incarnation of God (Luke 2:8-14).

Entering the scene were shepherds and angels…humans and celestial beings from the realm of glory. Going about their nightly duties, these shepherds of the temple flocks encountered a sobering and life-changing event. As they were watching over the sheep sleepily — suddenly an angel stood by them, and the glory of God — that radiating, brilliant splendor or majesty of God dazzled them. The Old Testament called it the "Shekinah glory" of God.

Their unexpected guest told them not to fear for he had wonderful, glorious news for them. He was there on God's behalf to tell them a secret. But the secret would soon be out for all the world to hear! He was there to tell them about the Savior….the one who would take away their sins…help them in their most desperate moments…who would save them from eternal hell…that Savior was being born that very night! He was the divine Savior the very incarnation of God himself.

We Christians firmly believe that the eternal second person of the triune Godhead joined himself with a complete human nature and was born as Jesus, the God-man. The apostle John wrote, "The Word became flesh and made his dwelling among us!" (John 1:14).

James Montgomery Boice's chapter in his book, *God the Redeemer*, stated that Paul also wrote about the incarnation. According to Boice, Paul traced Christ's life from eternity past, when he was in the form of God and equal to God through the events of his earthly life and eternity future, where he once again glorified with the father in Philippians 2:5-11. Boice said that Paul used two words in speaking of the position that Jesus enjoyed with the Father. The first is the Greek word, "morphe" found in the phrase, "the form of God." It referred to the internal fitness of the two together. As someone said, "(Jesus) possessed inwardly and displayed outwardly the very nature of God." The second word is "equal." It is like the isosceles triangle with two equal sides. It means that the two are equal. Jesus is fused as God and man in such a way that he became our one and only hope of salvation.

A legend is told about the casting of a great bell in Peking. It is the bell on which midnight is sounded, and it was cast a century and a half ago. Two attempts at casting were made and ended in failure. The emperor sent for Kuan-Yin, the official in charge of the task. The emperor informed Yin that if he failed again he would be killed. The legend continues that the man's daughter, Ko-ai, consulted an astrologer, who told her that unless a virgin's blood was mingled with the metal the third casting it, too, would fail. She asked permission to be present when the attempt was made. As her father and his helpers were rushing to get the white-hot metal from the furnace into the great mold the devoted daughter sprang forward with the cry, "For my father!" and leaped into the fiery stream adding her life-blood into its composition, and won her father's safety and success.

The unknown author of the story makes the spiritual application as he wrote that the great bell of humanity was out of tune. It swung gloomily and sadly, and its music was all harsh, grating, and discordant. Then our Savior threw himself from the heights of heaven. His life-blood entered into a world's alloy, and ever since, the vast bell has been growing sweeter and more attuned to the heavenly music for those who have found the redeemer.

III. Christmas is about sharing the story of God (Luke 2:15-20).

The shepherds journeyed to find the baby. At The Bethlehem Inn they found Mary, Joseph, and the focus of their search, Jesus. The Bible says that after they had seen the child, they spread the word concerning what had been told them...and all who heard it were amazed at what the shepherds said to them." They were truly the first evangelists of the gospel of Jesus!

That is our job once we have encountered this Jesus...incarnate God...Savior...we are to share with others the good news that we are loved by God. He has given his Son to us for our salvation!

They went back to the fields, back to being shepherds, back to the routine of life, but with a whole new perspective. This is true of us. Each year as we celebrate the joyous services, countless cantatas, the festive parties, all of the excitement and thrill of the season what have they done to change our lives? What difference will this Christmas mean when we go back to the lives we lead in our schools, jobs, homes and lives? If we believe the message of the angels we go back to the ordinary with a new focus...a better focus...a spiritual focus on Jesus!

Conclusion

Joseph Bayly wrote a wonderful poem about the meaning of Christmas. The last two lines inspired me years ago when I read it.

"I will sing praise to the infinite, eternal Son,

Who became most finite, a baby who would one day

Be executed for my crime.

Praise him in the heavens, praise him in the stable, praise him in my heart."

Friend, can you praise him? Do you know him? Is he your Christ, your Lord, your Savior? He wants to be. That's the reason he came into this world!

Amen.

First Sunday After Christmas Day
Luke 2:41-51

Don't Miss Jesus

Luke is the only gospel writer who gives us a peek into the childhood of Jesus. Luke, the physician, is analytical and an observer of life. Biblical historians believe that Luke had much of his research with first hand observers of the life, death and resurrection of Jesus. Not being an apostle or having first person knowledge, he relied upon others. One of those was Mary, the mother of Jesus.

Someone said that Jesus' childhood is like a walled garden — the inside of which no one has seen. Luke plucked one flower from inside that garden and gave it to us to read and contemplate. (Bruce Larson, *Communicator's Commentary*, p.61)

Let's examine the background of this scripture passage.

First: We read that the nuclear family of Joseph, Mary, and Jesus traveled to Jerusalem to celebrate the Passover Festival. Jewish rabbinical law required every male to go to three annual festivals a year in Jerusalem. When that was established it was much easier for the men to attend, but time and distance had eroded that possibility. The Jews were now scattered over many miles in the Roman Empire so that most attended only one of the festivals a year.

Second: The festival that the family attended traditionally was the Passover Feast Festival. This festival was a seven-day event celebrating the deliverance that God gave to the Israelites when Moses led them out of Egypt. The Passover was the tenth plague visited upon the Egyptians by God when the death angel passed throughout the land. Moses was told that blood from a lamb was to be placed on the door posts of the houses of the land and the angel would "pass over" them and their first born would live. It is this last plague that finally convinced Pharaoh to allow the Israelites to leave Egypt. The Israelites would continue to celebrate this festival of the exodus from slavery until this very day. Two thousand years ago Jesus and his family would remember the freedom their ancestors received.

Third: Luke told us that Jesus was twelve years old. This story occurred one year before Jesus' bar mitzvah. According to Jewish law a Jewish boy becomes an adult at age thirteen. That means he becomes accountable for his own actions or obligated to the ritual responsibilities of Jewish life. We discover through our reading that Jesus is already preparing himself for this important event in his life when he is in the temple listening and asking questions of the religious scholars.

What can we learn from today's scripture passage?

I.   We must be careful not to miss Jesus (Luke 2:43b).

The festival is over and the family is headed home to Nazareth. They are not a threesome like we would think today. The Jews of that time lived in extended families and for any travel to festivals they walked together as a whole caravan of people…friends and family. Men and women separately. Usually the younger children would walk with moms at the front of the caravan, but older children could go either direction between the two groups. The kids belonged to everybody! This lessened the threat from thieves and other dangerous situations along the road. It also gave time for fellowship.

As one commentator observed, the caravan could be joined by other groups of travelers from neighboring towns to form a great company of people moving from the foothills and deserts of the area. Mary thought Jesus was probably with Joseph while Joseph thought Jesus was with Mary. When they stopped for the night they met together. Mary probably was the first to ask, "Where is Jesus?" Joseph replied, "Isn't he with you?" A frantic search began and they found that no one had seen him since they left that morning. Luke 2:46 states that they looked for Jesus for three days. As Bruce Larson observed, it seems more logical to assume it took one day for the journey away from Jerusalem, one day to return back to the city, and one day to search for the boy.

These parents didn't abandon Jesus. It was an unfortunate mistake. They absolutely loved their son.

The Daily Guideposts for December 29, 2013 told that a young couple, Phil and Katie, who had three children of their own, decided to adopt a little girl who had been abandoned on the streets of China. The grandmother, Brenda Wilbee, was writing the devotional for the day and she said that before getting her, they learned that she had osteogenesis imperfect (brittle bone disease). Later on they learned that the diagnosis was much more serious than they were led to believe.

Brenda asked her son what they were going to do about the situation. With despair in his voice he shared, "I can't abandon her now." So the two-year-old was adopted. Several of her bones have since broken.

Surgeries have been a way of life for two-year old Alice. Phil's mom wrote, "I went to help out the day of (one) of her surgeries. Evidence of Phil and Katie's sacrifice for Alice was everywhere. Having given up their spacious two-story home, six people were jammed into a small fixer-upper. No privacy, no individual space, and no place to put coats or toys. They didn't seem to notice."

On that visit her grandson, Jamie, age seven, led her to where Alice lay on her mattress, leg splinted and waiting to travel to the hospital for surgery. The little girl gave a pain-laced smile to Brenda and Jamie. Alice and Jamie touched noses. Jamie said in a quivering voice, "It's so sad that she's so breakable...But what's not sad, Granny, is that she has such a cute face. Don't you think she has a cute face?"

Brenda wrote that she agreed with Jamie and that, "my heart was bursting with love for this joyous happy child — and overflowing with gratitude for her parents, unwilling to abandon her." (Daily Guidepost 2013, Guideposts New York, New York. P. 397)

Jesus may have been out of sight for a while from his parents, but never out of their hearts! They did everything to find him.

If you are missing Jesus, look for him. Abandon all else until you find Jesus. You can find him! He is at the edge of your heart waiting to come in today.

II. **We must be careful to look for and find Jesus (Luke 2:45-46).**

After returning to Jerusalem those parents looked frantically asking anybody and everybody who would listen if they had seen Jesus.

That is our goal…seeking Jesus…finding Jesus!

How do I seek God?

A. **By seeking calmness and serenity.**

We live in a chaotic and frightening world full of violence and marred by turmoil and conflict. Almost daily we see the aftermath of hatred, racism, and terror. It would be easy for us to hide from it or to fret over it or be in a constant state of fear. Only God can bring a peaceful, calm, and clear view when everything around us is swirling out of control. The prophet Isaiah stated it precisely, "You will keep him in perfect peace, whose mind is stayed on you, because he trusts in you" (Isaiah 26:3). The New Testament writer, John, quoted Jesus when he said, "Peace I leave with you, my peace I give to you; not as the world gives do I give to you. Let not your heart be troubled, neither let it be afraid" (John 14:27).

B. **By seeking purity of desire and heart.**

The beat of our heart ought to be like Jesus. We need to allow his Holy Spirit to fill us, and his love to overwhelm us. I want to act like Jesus, live as close to Jesus as possible, and seek his heart's desire for me!

C. **By seeking a spirit of cheerfulness and positive outlook.**

Listen to what God's Word says:

Philippians 4:8 (NIV) "Finally, brothers and sisters,

whatever is true, whatever is noble, whatever is right, whatever is pure, whatever is lovely, whatever is admirable — if anything is excellent or praiseworthy — think about such things."

Proverbs 4:6 (NIV) "Do not forsake wisdom, and she will protect you; love her and she will watch over you."

Jeremiah 29:11 (NIV) " 'For I know the plans I have for you,' declares the Lord, 'plans to prosper you and not to harm you, plans to give you hope and a future.'"

Matthew 14:27 (KJV) "Be of good cheer."

D.   By seeking a life of prayer.

Richard Baxter who lived in the 1600s wrote, "Prayer must carry on our work as much as preaching; he preacheth not heartily to his people, that will not pray for them." Prayer must precede all that ministers and laypersons do in the church. That includes teaching, serving on boards and committees, evangelizing, giving, and more.

How do I find Jesus? It is simple. Ask him to come into your life. Confess your need of him and that your sinfulness is more than you can handle. Thank him for his willingness to forgive you your sins. Serve him with your whole heart.

III.   We must be careful to live an obedient life (Luke 2:51-52).

Many of us are like the little boy who was confined for a time at a children's hospital many years ago. The child had gained a reputation for wreaking havoc with the staff and nurses. One day a visitor who knew about his terrorizing nature made him a deal: "If you are good for a week," she said, "I'll give you a dime when

I come again." A week later she stood before his bed. "I'll tell you what I won't ask the staff or the nurses if you behaved. You must tell me yourself. Do you deserve the dime?"

After a moment's pause, a small voice from under the covers said: "Gimme a penny."(The Tale of the Tardy Oxcart, Charles Swindoll, p. 413).

We compartmentalize our life. Religion is for Sunday. What we do with the rest of the week is ours. It's our words, our actions, our money, our (fill in the blank). The truth is that every compartment of our lives is Christ's.

Jesus said, "Anyone who loves me will obey my teaching. My Father will love them, and we will come to them and make our home with them" (John 14:23 NIV). We must be fully committed to obeying Jesus 100% of our lives. "Do not merely listen to the word, and so deceive yourselves. *Do* what it says" (James 1:22 NIV).

Mother Teresa of Calcutta once said, "Be faithful in the little practices of love which will build in you the life of holiness and make you Christlike." (Jan Karon, Patches of Light).

Conclusion

Hang on to the principles we were taught by Jesus and his family today. Remember that the essence of Christian living (holiness) as John Wesley said is simplicity and purity: one design, one desire: entire devotion to God.

Amen.

The Epiphany of Our Lord
Matthew 2:1-12

Walking In The Light

Four year old Billy was watching his mom change the diaper of his brand new baby brother. Mom was in a rush to get to her next appointment and forgot to put baby powder on the backside of the baby. As she turned to leave, Billy piped up, "Hey mom, you forgot to salt him!"

Babies have an extraordinary way of turning intelligent grown-ups into complete idiots as they make those funny noises and talk baby talk and make crazy faces. Have you ever wondered what the babies think about adults?

Christmas is the season of the baby, the Christ child. We have just come through the holy season of Christmas. The scripture however, isn't quite done with the Christmas season. God isn't locked into our calendar of events. The entrance of the wise men of Persia in the Christmas story brings a new dimension to the experience.

As you read about these Magi you discover they were members of the priestly caste of ancient Persia. They were followers of the Iranian prophet Zoroaster who taught messianism, heaven, hell, and free will and has been around since about 650 BC. There is much in the similarity of the Zorasterism and Christianity that was to come…except they expected a Messiah. Christianity delivers the Messiah. That is what the Magi were seeking…the Messiah…not a prophet.

The speaker of the International Lutheran Hour in the late 1980s gave a powerful introduction of the events that surrounded the appearance of the Magi. He said that the wise men of the east did not claim to know everything, but they did know that something wonderful was happening. They followed the star. He said, "I wish I knew how they did that. With what they knew, they were able to do it. Their studies paid off. They knew a special star when they saw it, and they were able to follow it."

The speaker continued with a question. "Why a star? Because a star had been born in Bethlehem. In a manger there, a little star from heaven had been born, as babies are born. The New Testament calls him a bright and blazing morning star, which heralds the dawn of a new day….God's new day in God's world."

They saw a bright star…a light…that would guide them by day and by night to the long expected Messiah…God's Messiah. Let's examine their journey.

The Magi took a journey of marked discovery.

These Magi were men of science in the field of astronomy who put their learning and feet into action. Someone called them "brave men" because they traveled by animal and foot hundreds of miles from home on the belief that their calculations were correct. They maneuvered over rough terrain and warded off bands of roving robbers just to see if they were correct about the star. It took them a long time to travel. When we see the manger scene in church plays and suddenly the Magi appear with their gifts…that is incorrect. Probably the star appeared at the time of Jesus birth and it is at that time they prepare to leave on their journey of discovery.

There was a widespread expectation of the coming of a great king, a deliverer. The Roman historian, Suetonius, was speaking around the time of the birth of Jesus about a ruler who would come from Judea. Tacitus, another Roman historian, wrote that there was a firm persuasion that a universal empire was going to be established. The Jewish historian Josephus reported in his Jewish Wars that the Jews believed that one from their own country would soon become ruler of the whole earth.

Whatever the case, these Magi were on a mission to find the *king*.

Bringing it to 2019, the question is what about us? What is our mission in life? Have we sought the king of life? Have we been involved with the continual search until we have found him? The baby grew up to become the man who would redeem the whole world. Not in the way that the Romans and Jews perceived, but he would redeem us from the world of sin and evil. Our search leads us past the baby to the victorious King of kings...the resurrected Lord of lords...to the Prince of Peace who has come to calm our fears, forgive our sins, and dispel the rebellion that has been brewing in you all of your life. Wise men and women still seek him. Brave people still join the army of the righteous and holy kingdom of God.

The Magi were on a journey marked with patience and persistence.

There had been that anticipation that something was about to happen in the ancient world. It would be something that would revolutionize the planet. There was a feeling in the air everywhere in the east. These men were watching and waiting. They were thinking and planning. They persistently had their eyes on the heavens to find out what it would be that would change their world.

I heard a story several years ago about a young Catholic boy named Benjamin. The child wanted a baby sister and decided the best way to do that was to ask God for one. He decided to write a letter to God asking for the new sister. He started the letter out:

"Dear God, This is Benjamin and I have been a very good boy." He stopped, thought about what he said and started over with a clean sheet of paper. He launched into the next start, "Dear God, This is Benjamin and most of the time I've been a good boy." Then he thought, "No, God won't believe that either." He wadded up his paper and threw it into the trash can.

He sat there thinking what he could do to convince God to give him a baby sister. An idea formed in his mind and then he took action. He went into the bathroom, grabbed a big terry-cloth towel, brought it into the living room and laid it on the couch. Then he went to the family fireplace mantle, reached up and brought down a statue of the Madonna, the mother of Jesus, that was sitting there all of his life.

Benjamin placed the statue in the middle of the towel, gently folded over the edges, and placed a spongy cord around it concealing its content. He brought it over to the table and took out another piece of writing paper and started his letter again. "Dear God, This is Benjamin and if you ever want to see your mother again…" Benjamin wanted God to act. He wanted God to act *now*.

We are often like Benjamin. We try to do desperate things to get God's attention. Most of us do not like to be patient and wait. Waiting drives us crazy!

One sharp person said, "I need to take a lesson in patience. Do you know where I can take a crash course?"

Someone told that in a certain orchestral number by Joseph Haydn, the flute player is supposed to sit quietly for 74 measures and then come in exactly on the upbeat of measure 75. Gerald Johnson, historian and writer, played the flute in the Baltimore symphony. He observed that a composer who expected a flute player to wait that patiently and perform that precisely is looking for a rare individual.

There are two kinds of realities in life…there are things you have to work for and things you have to wait on. How many of us don't want to wait?

I often feel like Phillips Brooks who was called the "Prince of Preachers" in the late 1800s. He was in his office pacing back and forth in a state of agitation. A friend asked him what was wrong. "He said, "I'm in a hurry, but God is not!"

It is hard for us when we aren't in control of things. Hurry! Hurry! Hurry! Isn't that the motif of our lives today? We must take our time and let God speak to us in his timing!

Once we have determined what his desire is we must take action. Have you waited on the Lord? Have you asked of him what he has in store for your life? Have you been persistent in your asking and once discovering what is to be done, persistent in your action? What is it today — now — that God wants for and from your life?

The Magi were on a journey marked faith.

When they took their first step on their journey it became a walk of faith. Millions of people since that time have experienced fellowship daily with an unseen God with whom they can experience only by faith. It is based on the inerrant Word of God, his revelation of himself to our world.

The Magi's faith was accompanied by their works... their action plan of moving out into the journey itself. Martin Luther is credited with the thought that, "Where there are no good works, there is no faith. If works and love do not blossom forth, it is not genuine faith, the gospel has not yet gained a foothold, and Christ is not yet rightly known." (Quoted from Jan Karon's, Patches of Godlight).

Here are some affirmations of faith:
- Faith affirms the truth that salvation and justification come by grace through faith in Christ (Romans 1:16).
- Faith affirms the truth that life is one of total trust from beginning to end (Galatians 2:20).
- Faith affirms the truth that faith will sustain believers in the trials and tribulations of life (1 Peter 1:5-7).
- Faith affirms the truth that faith gives victory to overcome the evil of this world (1 John 5:4-5).
- Faith affirms the truth that Christian growth is possible (1 Peter 1:5-8).
- Faith affirms the truth that prayer is vital in our lives for spiritual maturity (James 5:15).

God redeems us through our faith in him. Are you a person who will put your faith in a God who has put his signature on a covenant with you signed in Christ's blood? He will help us face every obstacle and challenge in life as we put our faith in his unlimited source of power! Faith that can move the mountains of doubt and fear!

The Magi were on a journey marked generosity.

They brought gifts to Jesus. Their conscience and hope would not be stingy, but generous to the one they searched so diligently for on their journey.

Gold represented his kingship, which would be one based on love and not force!

Frankincense represented his priesthood. The function of a priest is to bring humanity to God. The Latin word for priest is "pontifex," which means a "bridge-builder." That is what Jesus has done! We can come into the very presence of God. We need no human priest to accomplish that for us.

Myrrh is the gift for one who is to die. It was an embalming mixture. Jesus came into the world to die for our sins.

What do I have to present to Jesus? The answer is *me*!

Conclusion

The Magi returned home. I have been thinking about their encounter with the baby Jesus.

Did the encounter change the hearts of the Magi... short term? Long term?

Did the encounter change the outlook of the Magi?

Did the encounter change the religious perspective of the Magi?

Did the encounter change the routine back home of the Magi?

I cannot answer the questions. Nothing is told in scripture or literature what happened to them. Honestly, I don't have to answer the question. I have a more pressing question to answer. Has my encounter with this Jesus changed my life?

The Baptism of Our Lord
Luke 3:15-17, 21-22

The Baptism Of The Lord

Rummaging through some of my old memorabilia I rediscovered a post card with the picture of a church on it. I well remember the church because it was the one where I was baptized. As a child of eight I asked Jesus to come into my heart at the altar of my small local church. It was an important time in my life and it started me on my Christian walk. The small church where I put down my spiritual roots did not have a baptistry in it. My pastor told us that it was important for new Christians to be baptized because Jesus commanded it.

As a child I told my mother that I wanted to be baptized with others and she agreed to allow me to be baptized with my friends. Most people in my church believed that if you were to be baptized it had to be by immersion. I went along with the consensus. My desire was to be whatever Jesus wanted me to be and to do whatever he wanted me to do. On the appointed Sunday afternoon our little group of Christians drove over to the big church across town that allowed us to have our baptismal service. One by one we waded out into the baptismal tank as our pastor asked us to give our testimony of faith about Jesus. Once that happened each of us was immersed…baptized…in the faith of Jesus Christ.

My water baptism was almost 64 years ago. I have been through college, seminary, and decades of pastoral ministry as well as denominational administration. My theological understanding has matured and ripened over the decades. I have a better understanding of the theological controversy about the doctrine and practice of baptism. Listening to ministers from various denominations share their views has broadened my appreciation for each of their stances. But I have discovered that the common bond is the recognition of God's provision of his sacred salvation in each of their positions.

Personally, I have a deep appreciation for the sacrament of water baptism as a symbol of God's covenant with a young child of eight back in Kansas City all those years ago. His baptism is still my baptism of faith in what God has done for me through Jesus Christ. When John baptized Jesus it was a visible, outward sign signifying that the word may become our own experience.

This is what I believe baptism is to me. Maybe you'll be able to find some common ground with me in our search for greater understanding of our faith.

Baptism is a sign that my sins are forgiven (Acts 2:38).

Charles Spurgeon wrote, "Let us go to Calvary to learn how we may be forgiven. And then let us linger there to learn how to forgive."

Christians have learned that there is such a thing as "godly sorrow" as Paul wrote to the Corinthians (2 Corinthians 7:10). It goes to the heart of the matter that honest repentance both recognizes the horror of sin and guilt and yet recognizes the depth of the power of saving grace through transformation of life!

"The doctrine of God's gracious forgiveness, like all the other doctrines of grace, is grounded not only in the divine initiative (Jesus coming into the world) but, in God's expectation of our active and persisting response to his love." (Beacon Dictionary of Theology, p.223).

Forgiveness is our acceptance of the death and resurrection of Jesus and a changed life both theologically and practically.

We need to rejoice and maybe throw a party every time a sinner comes to God or a backslider returns to the fold!

Charles Swindoll told about a pastor who went through the public discipline of a brother in Christ in his local church. Years passed as the man walked away from God and the church. His life was a shipwreck of disgrace. Finally he realized what he had done through God's conviction and loving counsel from friends. He wrote a note of apology to the church, pastor, and friends of that congregation. He ultimately said he was wrong and he was living a sinful life. He had rebelled and rejected God and their discipline. He wrote, "I want you to know, I see the wrong of my actions and I've come back."

Swindoll asked, "Do you know what the church did?" They had a party — this same church that had disciplined him. They bought him a couple of gifts and had a prime rib dinner. It was an evening of praise as this brother was brought back into fellowship. Swindoll observed there's not enough of that kind of action by the church.

Forgiveness is setting the prisoner free...and the prisoner is *you*!

Baptism is a sign of my relationship with Christ (Galatians 3:26-38).

Paul wrote, "So in Christ Jesus you are all children of God through faith" (Galatians 3:26 NIV). When Jesus enters our hearts, he brings the fellowship of God into play. The grand motivation of this relationship is his love for us. John pens the reason for this relationship, "For God so loved the world that he gave his one and only Son, that whosoever believes in him shall not perish but have eternal life. For God did not send his Son into the world to condemn the world, but to save the world through him" (John 3:16-17 NIV). What's the benefit? God living in my heart without condemning me! This also provides a future life that begins now and continues on through eternity.

One night before the great Broadway musical star, Mary Martin, was to go on stage in South Pacific, a note was handed to her. It was Oscar Hammerstein, the American librettist, theatrical producer, and director of musicals from the 1920s to 1960, who wrote the lyrics for *South Pacific*. "Dear Mary, A bell's not a bell till you ring it. A song's not a song till you sing it. Love in your heart is not put there to stay. Love isn't love 'til you give it away." (James Hewett, Illustrations Unlimited).

God understood that and gave us his love so that we could enjoy his fellowship forever!

Baptism is a sign of fellowship with other believers (1Corinthians 12:13).

Baptism brings me into a holy fellowship by connecting me with others. When I was young the church I attended the people would call each other, "brother" or "sister." That tradition has been "outgrown" by a more sophisticated church culture. The truth is we really have become brothers and sisters if we are in Christ. We have a fellowship that the world cannot understand. Christ bonds us together as nothing else can do. If the church does not have Christ at the center, then it is no more than a service club.

The fellowship of believers has been likened to a hospital for those needing spiritual and moral healing. It is a place for us to come and share together in the hurts, difficulties and tragedies of life through Christ.

The fellowship of believers is the place where people gather to invite the presence of the Holy Spirit to empower them to live holy, righteous, caring, loving lives together.

The fellowship of believers is to light the fire under one another to carry out the mission that Christ gave us, "Go and make disciples of all nations, baptizing them in the name of the Father and of the Son and of the Holy Spirit, teaching them to obey everything I have commanded you. And surely I am with you always, to the very end of the age" (Matthew 28:18-19 NIV).

The fellowship of believers is to be engaged in the life of the community. We are not to withdraw from the world we live in and become monastics or isolationists. As you observe the life of Jesus he continually engaged in meeting the needs of the world through healing, giving hope, breaking the caste system (think of the Samaritan woman, the tax collectors like Zacchaeus and Matthew), changing the moral culture of his society, and challenging the arrogant Pharisees. What are we doing to make a difference in our world as the fellowship of believers? How are we engaging in our community?

Paul wrote to the church of Galatians, "You, my brothers and sister, were called to be free. But do not use your freedom to indulge the flesh, rather, serve one another humbly in love. For the entire law is fulfilled in keeping this one command: 'Love your neighbor as yourself'" (Galatians 5:13-14 NIV).

Here are a few thoughts.
- Open up a free clinic in the community. Hire a parish nurse to help out the needs of the elderly.
- Provide free babysitting for mothers during the day.
- Make a jail ministry a priority.
- Have a counseling center for those in need.
- Open up the church for community meetings.
- Have free car washes at community festivals.
- Provide housing for the homeless.
- Help the hungry by providing free food or community soup nights.
- Ask the congregation to come up with other ideas.

Lighthouses are a passion for me. The reason is their function over the years. These lighthouses saved the lives of seaman by lighting the way over dangerous seacoasts. As a church our task is to help those who are navigating the dangerous coasts of life as we help light the way to safety. We do it as a group…a team…a body of saved individuals who have been rescued by the Savior, Jesus!

Conclusion

Matthew Henry was an English minister and Bible commentator who lived from 1662-1714. His father's name was Philip and he wrote a baptismal statement that has been quoted often. The statement reads:

> *I take God to be my chief and highest good.*
> *I take God the Son to be my prince and Savior.*
> *I take God the Holy Spirit to be my sanctifier, teacher, guide, and comforter.*
> *I take the word of God to be my rule in all my actions and the people of God to be my people under all conditions.*
> *I do hereby dedicate and devote to the Lord all that I am, all that I have and all I can do.*
> *And this I do deliberately, freely, and forever. Amen.*

(Quoted in protevangelium.blogspot.com).

Epiphany 2
John 2:1-11

Jesus Meets Our Needs

Weddings symbolize the hope of the future for people who are in love. They symbolize to commitment, undying love and the best in each other's company. It is at such an occasion that the first miracle of Jesus happened.

The wedding took place in Cana of Galilee not far from Nazareth. It is the small village where Nathanael lived and he is the one who had said, "Can anything good come from there?" (John 1:46). Cana and Nazareth obviously were rival communities. Yet, it is here that Jesus, his disciples and his mother attended this celebration.

According to ritual custom and Jewish law, if the bride was a virgin the wedding took place on a Wednesday and if she were a widow then it would take place on Thursday. The wedding of that era was a lengthy celebration. They didn't just meet at the church for a thirty minute ceremony and a dinner the same day. Rather, it was a week-long event.

The day of the actual wedding ceremony there was a feast and after the meal there would be a procession through the village streets with laughter, music, dancing, jokes, and loud fun! Later in the evening the wedding ceremony took place, but our text takes us to the feast. John sees a deep rich message for his readers in this marriage event. Roger Fredrikson in the Communicator's Commentary on John wrote, "That intimate relation between Yahweh and Israel is portrayed over and over again through the image of the marriage covenant (Hosea 2:7). The fullness of the messianic age was prophesied in Isaiah and spoken of so beautifully through the symbol of marriage (Isaiah 62:5), and the vision of the consummation of all history will be celebrated in the marriage of the 'Lamb and his wife' when glory is given the Lord-God omnipotent (Revelation 19:7 NIV)." Fredrikson went on to suggest, "How highly suggestive then that Jesus' first miracle, inaugurating the messianic age, should be the sign given at a wedding." (pp.67-68).

Jesus becomes the answer to our needs both here and for eternity. The text helps us understand how that occurs.

I. Mary discovered a need (John 2:1-3).

Some think that this was a family wedding and that the groom was a relative of Mary. No one knows for sure, but it is an interesting theory. There is the thought that Mary was the wedding coordinator for the occasion, because she was the one who directed the wine stewards to follow Jesus' lead (John 2:5). Mary determined that there was a need and that something had to be done quickly so that the wedding host would not be embarrassed. The Jewish rabbis would say, "Without wine there is no joy." According to Barclay the composition of the wine was two parts wine and three parts water. This was a matter of social etiquette and hospitality. It was a holy duty in the East if such provisions were not given. Since this was a week-long affair somehow the wine supply was decimated. Mary notices there were six twenty-gallon containers which meant 120 gallons of wine was gone and needed to be resupplied.

Sometimes we overlook the needs that are right around us.

- How many people go hungry around your neighborhood?
- How many homeless and neglected children are living in their cars or under bridges near your home or church?
- How many people around the area are addicted and need someone to help pull them up out of the muck of life?
- How many senior adults are lonely, shadows on the wall of humanity, and no one cares?

Look around and discover the needs that are in your reach!

II.   Mary recruited help for the need (John 2:4-8).

As wedding coordinator, Mary made the determination that help was needed. She turned first to her son and then to the servants attending the event. For many, verse four in the King James Version has always seemed harsh. "Woman, what have I to do with thee?" Other translations have attempted to catch the tone, as well as the actual wording. William Barclay helped me to grasp the intent of the phrase when he wrote that the meaning of what Jesus was saying to Mary was, "Don't worry; you don't quite understand what is going on; leave things to me and I will settle them in my own way." Then Mary directed the servant to do whatever it would be that Jesus would tell them to do. He told them to fill the jars to the top with water.

Perceptibility of need was great, but it was only half of the story. Action was needed.

Here are some ideas about recruiting people to help in the church.

- Be specific. Notice what Mary said, "Do what he tells you" (John 2:5 NIV). Jesus is specific to the servants: "Fill the jars with water" (John 2:7 NIV). "Now draw some out and take it to the master" (John 2:8). Often we are vague in what we want people to do in the church. What they need is a clear vision of what is wanted — how to accomplish the task. Who would help them if they needed help? When is the task to start and end?
- Expect the end result to be satisfactory, but be realistic. Lugging those six twenty-gallon jugs around was not easy, but the result was terrific. After tasting the water turned to wine, the master of the banquet said, "Wow, this is the best yet. Everyone starts with the best and ends with the least quality, but you have reversed it. You have saved the best for last" (Keefer translation).
- Let me show you. Jesus took the time to show the servants where the large containers were and gave the specific directions on what to do. If we want people to follow in our steps as disciples we need to become mentors to them. That includes family and friends in the broader sense of mentoring as well. People will feel like part

of a team, relationships, or job from the start as they are mentored.
- Work together. Mary, Jesus, and the servants tag-teamed to make this miracle a success. We can work together to make the spiritual experience, the church, family life a total success is by each one pulling together in a positive motivational venture.

An *Upper Room* daily devotional titled, Live In Harmony by Maria M. Urdaz de Rosario from Puerto Rico described a particular type of bird that lived in the Kalahari Desert in Africa. They are called "sociable weaver birds" who erect very large and inviting nest to house hundreds of birds on trees and other tall objects. These nests insulate the birds from the extreme cold or heat of the desert.

Maria wrote that the birds shared their food, worked as a team in mending their nests, and allowed all varieties of birds to live in their colonies. Peace and harmony was the desired end. (The *Upper Room* daily devotional is an online publication. Google *The Upper Room*).

Our action in recruiting others is to help them to work together for the good of the church, the kingdom of God, society, and family. How is your action helping to make that happen?

III. Mary knew the answer to the need (John 2:5)

Mary knew her son. Thirty years of living with him instilled a sense of who he was in life. There would be a time when she questioned his focus (Matthew 12:46-50; Luke 8:19-21). That was later, but for now she knew the answer to the need of making everyone satisfied… Jesus!

There are moments in life when everything turns black. The road ahead is not discernable. Recently one of the ladies of the congregation I serve lost her mother first and then her dad. A short time later her husband died after a long illness. The last personal hurricane was the death of her adult daughter. Her words haunt me, "I hurt so badly, pastor. I feel so at a loss." I struggle to counsel her. Words seem so empty. The platitudes and phrases meaningless. The only hope I have...her only hope is to put her faith in Christ. With his help she could find the right grief support program...friends who could listen...people who cared...words from God found in the Bible that would instill a trust and faith...a loving congregation who would surround her and not let her fall or be lonely.

Jesus leads us to God who gives us eternity's answers to our needs. It is in his purpose, his will, and his direction that each of us must find the answer to the needs we have in life!

Final thought

Barclay said it so well, "No need on earth can exhaust the grace of Christ. There is a glorious superabundance in the grace of Christ." The grace has become so limitless and more, than sufficient for every need. When Jesus comes into our lives, he makes our lives quality! He sparkles and shines and exhilarates us. Our spiritual lives can take on a heavenly glow!

What need do you have today? Turn it over to Jesus, the author of grace, who meets all our needs! Praise be to God!

Amen.

Epiphany 3
Luke 4:14-21

Jesus In Ministry — Us In Ministry

Chuck Swindoll illustrates how ministry concerns all of us in his "Saving Lives" parable (https://www.insight.org of October 2, 2015).

On a rugged section of seacoast many decades ago a crude lifesaving station was built. Only a few volunteers manned the station to watch for ships that were in danger of the rocks. On the occasion of a shipwreck the handful of volunteers took their one and only boat out to bring others to shore safely. The number of saved sailors soared as the lifesaving station gained in status because of the dramatic rescues.

As the reputation increased more people wanted to be a part of the life-saving experience. The few volunteers became many. People poured in resources and support to make changes in the station. The crude hut became a beautiful building replete with the most comfortable and luxurious furnishings. A gradual shift of emphasis occurred. The immediacy of saving lives was downplayed as the station took on more of a clubhouse feel. One had to be a member with paid dues to be a part of the crew. A few of the volunteers were still manning the boats, but because of the size and number they had to be augmented with professionals hired by the membership. Most of the life-saving members didn't want the responsibility of going out to sea to rescue people. "Why bother?" was their motto.

A luxury cruiser was wrecked not far from the station and the crews went out and brought back the half-drowned people. The problem was they were wet, dirty, messy, and created a horrible disaster inside the clubhouse. Their messiness created a mess! This was unthinkable.

At the next meeting there was an uproar. A division resulted after angry words were spoken with feelings hurt and bruised. A few wanted to stick to the purpose of the original station...saving lives. The majority wanted the clubhouse feel which excluded messes and people. Those who wanted to stay with the life-saving purpose were voted down and told to start their own station...down the coast and not to close to the club. The clubhouse members lost their servant hearts to a different mentality and purpose. Their entire purpose to serve and care about the victims was drowned with their ministry to others.

Today's scripture lesson on ministry illustrates the servant heart of Jesus. His heartbeat must pump inside each person who claims to be a disciple of Christ. Servanthood is our watchword.

I. Christ's ministry reached out to the poor of the community (Luke 4:18a).

Most people who knew Jesus were hurting financially. Their meager earnings kept them in an economical prison that was difficult to overcome. Like many world areas today the governmental and religious leadership seemed to overlook their plight. They exploited their circumstances by keeping a strangled hold on them and pushed them deeper into poverty.

The poor seemed to be shadows on the wall of life. Nothing was done to reach down to help pull them out of their situation. Christ boldly proclaimed the good news to the poor. He came to help them see the richness of a better life.

During my college career I attended a Christian college that believed in social justice and evangelizing the poor. I participated in a group with a mission's emphasis. Traveling a few miles from the campus we made our way to one of the poorest neighborhoods in our community. Some lived in cardboard boxes, others in burned out busses, while some lived in small, but neat little wooden structures that were well kept. We discovered that though some couldn't afford the wooden structures they chose to live in their makeshift "homes." The families who lived in their neat little houses and yards were families who had come to know and experience Christ in their lives. What gave me a lasting impression that day was that these people had a self-esteem that developed from their relationship with Jesus. I understood that Christ took the "poor me" out of them and replaced it with a "rich me" in the heart. Still poverty stricken…still with financial problems…they had a new outlook and perspective. Their "richness" was in themselves and the Christ who they loved.

We still have the poor with us. The immigration from world areas continues to grow whether in France, Britain, the United States, or Germany. Poor people who are less fortunate, struggling financially, needing a hand up will continue to pour into our lands and we who claim to be Christians must not turn a deaf ear or a helping hand away.

What can we do? We cannot feed the entire world, give everyone a job, make poverty go away, but we can offer some positive help!

- Ask what can be done to help the poor in your community, your church, your world. The Egyptian Jesuit, Henri Boulard wrote, "What we lack is not time, but heart." (Jan Karon, *Patches of Godlight*, New York, Penguin Books, 2001).
- Find legitimate organizations that care about people in need to give to, including your local church!
- Volunteer to help through church missions programs, senior citizen's groups, rescue missions, food pantries, soup kitchens or other ministry oriented organizations that are reaching out.
- Christ's ministry reached out to the spiritually oppressed (Luke 4:18 b).

Christ's concern for the poor reached deeper than just financial or social issues in life. It went to the heart of the problem...the spiritual. As the redeemer, Jesus called those that day back to a full restoration. Those sitting in the synagogue needed their stomachs filled, but what they needed more was their spiritual appetite satisfied. Christ would do that by taking the emptiness of sin away and letting them feast on the satisfying buffet of righteousness.

We need that freedom! The time of letting sin go and let righteousness come in through the person of Jesus!

Sin destroys...righteousness restores.

Sin holds us spiritually powerless in its grip...righteousness gives us power through the Holy Spirit.

Sin makes us selfish...righteousness unleashes the unselfishness inside.

Sin limits...righteousness frees.

Sin destines us to eternal punishment...righteousness to eternal life.

Why be spiritually oppressed when we can be free?

Six years after the Civil War, Dwight L. Moody stood in his Chicago church and preached to a large congregation a sermon entitled, "What Will You Do Then with Jesus Who I Called the Christ?" His strenuous workload had exhausted his physical and mental life. At the end of his message he did something that he regretted the rest of his life. The power of the message was evident to everyone that night, but instead of giving them an opportunity to make a decision for Christ he said, "Now I give you a week to think this over. And when we come together again, you will have opportunity to respond.

Music Minister, Ira Sankey, stood and began singing, but before he finished the song sirens were blaring their warning sounds in the streets of Chicago. The great fire of Chicago had begun and before it was over one hundred thousand people were homeless and people by the hundreds died in the fire. Months later Dwight Moody rose to the occasion and said, "I would give my right arm before I would ever give an audience another week to think over the message of the gospel. Some who heard me that night died in the fire."

Christ's ministry was to come and to save the spiritually oppressed. Today, you have a decision to make. Will you take Jesus at his word and let him come in and free you from your sin?

II. Christ's ministry opened the eyes of the blind (Luke 4:18c).

I read with interest the story of Rose Crawford who had been blind for fifty years. After successful eye surgery and the healing process the doctor lifted her bandages from her eyes. Crawford gasped in disbelief and shouted, "I just can't believe it!" For the first time in her life in that Ontario hospital she saw the beautiful dazzling world of form and color. The sad part of the story is that twenty years of her blindness had been unnecessary. She didn't know that surgical procedures had advanced, and that an operation could have restored her vision at the age of thirty! When asked why she didn't have the operation sooner it was the doctor who said, "She just figured there was nothing that could be done with her blindness. Much of life could have been different!"

The illustrator writer asked some pointed questions. Why did she continue to assume that her situation was hopeless? Why hadn't someone told her about the new developments in operation procedures? Why did she finally ask for help? The author commented, "How many will go on living in moral blindness unless we bring them to the Savior? Millions will never know anything but spiritual darkness because no one has shared with them the light that has come into the world. (www.biblestudytools.com Unnecessarily Blind).

One of my favorite hymns by Philip Bliss that says,

The whole world was lost in the darkness of sin;
The light of the world is Jesus.
Like sunshine at noonday his glory shone in;
The light of the world is Jesus."

Come to the light; 'tis shining for thee.
Sweetly the light has dawned upon me.
Once I was blind, but now I can see.
The light of the world is Jesus.

(in the Public Domain)

What a wonderful thought in a world blindly going about its own thing...hatred, strife, envy, destruction, murder, terrorism, and more. On a very personal note, if your world is filled with darkness, the last phrase of that song is for you... "The light of the world is Jesus. "Come to the light...Come to Jesus!

Conclusion

If you are spiritually hungry, spiritually oppressed, spiritually blind...come to Jesus...*now*. Paul wrote to the Corinthians, "...I tell you, now is the time of God's favor, now is the day of salvation" (2 Corinthians 6:2 NIV).

Amen.

Epiphany 4
Luke 4:21-30

Rejecting The Message — Rejecting The Person

Jesus wanted people to know and experience his loving Father — the true God. Anything else was false love....false gods. Christ's message came directly from the heart of God. He and the Father were so intimately connected in heart, soul, and spirit.

His whirlwind preaching and teaching tour in the synagogues in the communities of the region of Galilee landed him in his own hometown of Nazareth. His celebrity status brought in the crowds on that powerful Saturday. The liberal minded people of Galilee were captivated by the ideas, thoughts, and innovative creative sermons of Jesus. He was viewed as a forward thinking preacher and the people were starving for a word from God. Jesus was the person to give it to them, but they were not ready to accept the hard truth of the message.

When the leader of the synagogue known as the Chazzam turned the service over to Jesus who came forward and sat in the "preaching chair" and read from the Isaiah scroll, Jesus launched into his sermon and people felt that he was doing an excellent ministry of preaching (Luke 4:22). Suddenly the atmosphere inside the building darkened. Anger surfaced to a boiling point? Why? What was the cause? The obvious reason was the compliment that he paid to Gentiles. The Jews believed that they were God's exclusive people. Anyone else was just fuel for hell's fire. Jesus had the audacity to include these Gentiles in God's kingdom… their exclusive God…Gentiles…no way!

Don't forget these were Jesus' friends and neighbors who had known him for years and many of them since childhood. These friends and neighbors were so incensed that they seized him and took him outside the synagogue to a cliff, and ready to throw him to his death. According to scripture he walked through the crowd and left. I don't know if this is a miracle or not, but he escaped with his life!

And what was the consequence of Jesus and his message being rejected by the Nazarene community? He never returned to his hometown to minister in God's name! What a devastating consequence!

What is our reaction to Jesus and his message?

I. **When they rejected Jesus and his message, they were rejecting the ministry of compassion.**

My grandmother gave her hard-earned money to a charlatan minister when I was a teenager. His message proclaimed that the more money you sent to his ministry, the more God would bless you and in time would make you a rich person. A portion of the ministry maintained that the more money you gave, God was obligated to "heal you from any infirmity that you had."

I grew up knowing his name and his ministry. My freshman year at college the evangelist and his team came to town. They set up their "faith healing service" in a large rented auditorium downtown.

His antics in the name of the Lord Jesus were appalling, yet so many believed that he had the special gift of healing. People packed the 2,000 seat auditorium to be healed because they were in pain, hurting, lonely, seeking for someone to relieve them of their ailments. Sitting there the music grew louder and more intense as the evangelist got more animated. A large curtain separated a group of people who had various needs such as blindness, deafness, leg, or knee injuries that required crutches. Each one came from behind the curtain and every time the healer touched them they could begin miraculously to see, hear, or throw away their crutches. It was a dramatic scene! Two of my friends had earlier gone behind the curtain before the healing service began. They were caught and thrown out of the area. Later they reported that the people in need of "healing" were waiting in the back, smoking, talking, and laughing. Not one of them was in need of healing. They were part of the show. Sadly, it was all for the sake of money.

Years later the evangelist and his ministry went up in smoke. He died of liver cancer from alcoholism and his miraculous team disappeared.

Matthew wrote that Jesus had great compassion on people, unlike the charlatan evangelist healer of my college youth. Jesus not only preached and taught; but the Bible stressed his healing ministry among the sick people on his Galilean tour. His ministry was restoring individuals to wholeness both spiritually and physically. His action showed mercy and compassion.

As congregations, we have the responsibility to show compassion to a world in deep need of Jesus. We accomplish this through the power of the Holy Spirit working in us and through us.

We need to become creative in thinking of ways to be compassionate as congregations. Here are some ideas that my congregation does in our small community.

- A Blessing Box: A wooden shelving unit where we put non-perishable items so that the homeless or those needing food can take freely.
- Volunteering at local community ministries: A Soup Pot that feeds the hungry two days a week.
- Support of local pregnancy agencies.
- An organization that strives to help those around the world earn a fare wage.
- Organizations that give away clothing.
- A local group that works with small farmers and sustainable food organizations.

There are reading programs at local schools. Hospital volunteers are needed. There are local fire departments that are looking for help.

What can your church do to be a compassionate congregation?

II. **When they were rejecting Jesus and his ministry they were rejecting the ministry of kindness.**

The ministry of kindness develops around individual responses to life. The story is told that when William McKinley was president of the United States, a decision about an appointment of an ambassador to a foreign country had to be made. Two equally qualified candidates were being considered. However, when McKinley was a congressman an incident occurred that would sway his decision. One of the candidates had been on the same streetcar at rush hour as McKinley. All of the seats were taken and eventually an elderly lady boarded the streetcar with a large and heavy basket of clothes. No one offered her a seat as the car swayed from side to side causing her to lose her balance more than once. She was standing next to one of the men that was being considered for the ambassadorship years later. Instead of getting up and offering her his seat he deliberately shifted his newspaper so it would look like he hadn't noticed her. When McKinley saw this, he walked down the aisle and took her basket and offered her his seat. The other man was unaware that anyone was watching, but his total lack of kindness would later cost him the job he so dearly desired! (www.sermonsearch.com).

The scriptures are filled with acts of kindness from the hands of Jesus from healing to the raising of the dead. His words encouraged people to see themselves for who they really were such as the woman at the well in Samaria (Luke 4:4-42). His disciples followed his example (Acts 3:1-10; Acts 4:32-37; Acts 5:12-16).

Modern day disciples need to be aware of kindness opportunities that God gives them.
- Find opportunities to give compliments. Everyone needs an encouraging word from the youngest to the oldest of people.
- At family reunions, church events, team sporting meetings, small group meetings, or any gathering give them a piece of paper with everyone's name on it and then have each person

write something they appreciate about that person.
- Bite your tongue. Don't say anything bad about people.
- Send "I missed you" cards to people who have been absent from church for a period of time. Don't forget to send to young children and teens!
- Extend a helping hand. If someone is overwhelmed with health issues, new baby, an accident, or whatever, call and extend a helping hand for a period of time...an hour, a day, a week.
- Make calls to local seniors after a major storm to assure they are doing okay or if they are in need.

Rabbi Harold Kushner said, "When you carry out acts of kindness, you get a wonderful feeling inside. It is as though something inside your body responds and says, 'Yes, this is how I ought to feel.'" (Quoted in Jan Karon's book, *Patches of Godlight*, see above).

III. **When they were rejecting Jesus and his ministry, they were rejecting the Godly true expectations.**

The Israelites' expectation of the coming Messiah was one of anticipation of a Messiah who would ride in on a white charger and lead a victorious army by defeating the hated Romans. Israel would be restored to its rightful and most powerful political position. Little did they dream that Jehovah would send them himself in the form of a man who would walk the dusty streets rather than ride a white horse? He would tell his followers to be peacemakers and love others above themselves and to render unto Caesar those things that he required. These things just didn't fit the ideal Messiah and yet that is exactly the kind of Messiah they received!

Today much of the world has a false expectation and understanding of Jesus...of the Messiah...of God. Where is this God who allows war, terrorism, divorce, illness, hatred, and more? If I ask Christ into my life, what realistic expectations should I have of him? Here is a short list. You can add more.

- I expect that during the rough and tumble times of life he will walk with me giving me encouragement, hope, understanding, and wisdom.
- I expect that he will provide an opportunity for me to draw upon his strength and power by pouring his Holy Spirit in my life.
- I expect that Jesus would extend a helping hand and bless ministries and endeavors that I will participate in for his glory.
- I expect that at the end of my life he will take me to heaven.

I do not want to be one who rejects Jesus, but my desire is to accept him and his ministry into my life that I might give him all the glory and honor that is due almighty holy God!

Amen.

Epiphany 5
Luke 5:1-11

Christ's Call To Discipleship

Throughout my academic career I struggled. Nothing came easily, but I determined to be the best pupil possible. The Greek culture considered a disciple a philosopher's follower or sometimes an apprentice learning a trade. The New Testament writers used the term in different facets. Don Campbell shared the uses of the word disciple in *The Theological Wordbook* as:

First, describing the twelve. Radical demands were placed on these men as Jesus was always on the move. He constantly challenged, motivated, questioned, and sharpened them into men who would eventually suffer for him and, for most of them, die for him! They were men who left their occupations, parents, families, friends to follow him. They learned from him the spiritual and social lessons that led to an unfolding of the drama of the redemption story.

Secondly, in the broadest sense of the word a disciple included all who believed in Jesus's words (John 8:30-31) and grappled with the truths he proposed. Luke 6:17 relates that there was a large number of disciples who represented a cross section of society. Unfortunately, they were surface disciples and when the teaching interfered with their lifestyle by becoming too difficult — they defected (John 6:60-66). Jesus expected true followers to accept his teachings and wholeheartedly fulfill the call to accept, believe and repent. The other expectation was to make other disciples.

Thirdly, the goal of discipleship is Christlikeness. We need to allow the Holy Spirit to hone us into the character of Jesus through conviction and our willingness change through the transforming power of God.

After leaving the synagogue of Galilee, Jesus ventured out to the lakeshore and used a boat for his pulpit. Christ went anywhere people that people would listen. His desire was to see lives changed.

One day I received an unusual phone call from a woman who asked to speak to the pastor. I assured her that I was the pastor of the local congregation and then asked what I could do for her. She bluntly said, "I want to be a member of your church." I thought this unique. I had never met the lady, she had never been inside my church, and I discovered through our phone conversation that she knew absolutely nothing about the church I pastored. She had no clue about our doctrines, beliefs, theology, policy, or history. Continuing on, she informed me that she didn't intend to attend the church or give financially, but simply felt a need to belong to a church and wanted me to take her into membership over the phone.

I shared with her that she needed a relationship with Jesus, a commitment to involvement, and a desire to bring others to Christ. Needless to say, she decided to forgo her membership in my local church.

Unfortunately, too many people are like the lady who called. They want to be "long distance" disciple. Discipleship demands involvement.

I. Christ's call to discipleship involves listening.

Paying attention to a person involves a conscious effort to hear and understand what is being said. In his book Gary Fenton, *Good for Goodness' Sake,* writes, "Listening is not only a means of gathering information, it is the way we acknowledge that the speaker has worth and value. The people with whom you have a good relationship are probably those who have listened to you. It was not important whether or not they could repeat back to you verbatim what you said, but the value was they validated you by listening."

When the crowds gathered around Jesus they listened because of his apparent authority. They were surprised and amazed with his incredible authoritative preaching. His sermons were rich in wisdom, grace, and direct simplicity aimed at their level of understanding. His illustrative material caught their attention because it came from where they lived daily. Love, sympathy, and concern pour freely as the wine from the large open containers at the wedding of Cana. His truth was like a sharp two-edged sword that cut deep into their hearts and soul. Certainly that caught the attention of the people to want to know and experience God! When Christ spoke, people listened!

As God speaks we must make a conscious effort to hear what is being said. Don't let other sounds drown out his voice. What competes for our listening ears?
- The burdens and cares of this world
- The rumblings of commerce that affects our finances
- The noise of jobs
- The luring sound of entertainment and pleasure
What are some of the ways we listen to God?

- Read his word. Get familiar with the Bible. God gave his holy word to be read and understood.
- Being available for service. Action is part of our spiritual listening process.
- Let your conscience be God's avenue to reach you.
- Allow the Holy Spirit to lead your activities.
- Prayer is the natural avenue of listening.

What is God saying to you?

II. Christ's call to discipleship involves an encounter with God.

Apparently Peter, James, and John were not paying attention to the preaching service that was going on around them. They were oblivious to Jesus as they were washing their nets (Luke 5:2).

Jesus caught Peter's attention by asking him to use his boat and requested a shove out into the water. Probably Peter wanted to make sure his boat was going to be safe, so he got on board with Jesus and was a captive audience as Jesus continued his teaching and preaching. Peter encountered the Lord of life. Whether the meeting was intentional on Christ's part or total unintentional we will never know, but it was so effective. It would change Peter's life forever.

Jesus seeks an encounter with us. He patiently waits for our willingness to meet him. What is it that has our attention over Christ? Are we too busy making a living, investing in the stock market, looking for the tricks of life, or running in circles? Stop! Look up and see Jesus calling your name asking if he can get on board of your boat on life's water.

Center stage to our discipleship encounter are the disciplines of life. Reaching our greatest potential in life is allowing God's disciplines to shape and sharpen us. Many years ago Richard Foster wrote a book titled *Celebration of Discipline*. Each discipline became a chapter in his book and a strong reminder that we have the choice and ability to become stronger disciples of Jesus.

Included were the inward disciplines such as meditation, prayer, fasting, and scriptural study. He characterized the outward disciplines as simplicity, solitude, submission and service. He shared the corporate disciplines as confession, worship, guidance, and celebration. Foster reminded his readers that just knowing the mechanics of discipline did not mean that they were practicing the particular discipline.

When a sculptor begins a project, they start with a blank block of statuary material. Chiseling, hammering, and honing the piece of marble, it becomes a piece of artwork. When we begin the disciplines we are only a block of spiritual statuary, but by the time God is done with us we can be a beautiful piece of spiritual artwork. It will take a lifetime. Will you begin, today?

III. Christ's call to discipleship involves willing obedience.

Reading the text, there is hesitancy on Peter's part when Jesus asked him to go out a little farther in the lake to let the nets down. Can you catch the reluctance and the frustration in Peter's voice as he responded to Christ's request? Can you hear it in your own voice when Christ asks you to respond to one of his requests? "Master, we have toiled *all* night and took *nothing!*" (Luke 5:5a RSV). Through gritted teeth and a whiney voice Peter responded, "but at your word I will let down the net" (Luke 5:5b RSV).

I am so much like Peter. How often I think, "I really don't want to do this." Then I say to the Lord, "But I will."

God wants to do so much with us, in us, through us, but we are too often reluctant and sometimes unwilling to do it. Following Christ in obedience is to walk along behind, watch, and observe. As we follow we have determined to learn from him by gathering strength, courage, information and desire. Dietrich Bonhoeffer wrote, "The disciple simply burns his boats and goes ahead. He is called out, and has to forsake his old life in order that he may 'exist' in the strictest sense of the word. The old life is left behind and completely surrendered. The disciple is dragged out of his relative security into a life of absolute insecurity…out of the realm of the finite…into the realm of infinite possibilities…it is nothing else than bondage to Jesus Christ alone." (Quoted from *The Cost of Discipleship* pp. 62-63).

Final thoughts

Our goal as Christians is to be followers of Christ. He brings security. Jesus redeems you from the cesspool of life or a life of disobedience. Today, he is ready to bring you to the heights of spiritual life. He has promised never to leave us nor forsake us (1 Peter 5:7). Show your great love for him as he shows you his great love personally. Be his disciple by simply being his follower!

Amen.

Epiphany 6
Luke 6:17-26

Rules For Basic Living

Rules! Rules! Rules! We have a love/hate relationship with them. They bring order to chaos...stability from unpredictability...soundness to erratic changes. However, rules can frustrate, overwhelm and discourage us because we view them as concrete, never-bending or always rigid. At times we resist them with a passion while at other times we embrace them with vitality.

How often has this conversation been played by a parent to their child?

Parent: "I told you not to do that, it's a rule in our house!"

Child: "Why?"

Parent: "Because I said so."

Maybe the parent doesn't really know, but their parent had the same conversation with them!

Often when we attempt to lay down those concrete rules, they are met with remarkable resistance. Bruce Larson tells the story that one day while shopping at a local department store, a teenager was overheard telling the clerk, "I love this outfit, but may I exchange it if my mom happens to like it?" Larson commented, "We all know that feeling. Somehow when someone in authority wants to guide us in matters of dress or behavior; we're a little rebellious." Can anyone here relate?

I think the basic problem is that we have been told "to do" or "not to do" without any explanation. I grew up in a conservative evangelical denomination that said "No" to dancing (even non-contact square dancing), smoking, drinking, cussing, movies, and before my lifetime, circuses, professional baseball games, bowling, billiards, and more. Having a desire to be an authentic Christian I refrained from those activities that were "nos" in my day. After all, a rule is a rule.

My denomination has evolved over the years and most of the rules are gone, but not without grief. If leadership on the local level would have explained the reasons, what a difference it could have made in the lives of its young people. Maybe that is why Jesus got in trouble with the Pharisees so often, because they said "do" or "don't do" just because it was a rule and not a life style endeavor that would lead to real life. Instead of drawing up an elaborate system of rules, if we stuck to the moral fiber and ethics that the Bible taught us it would revolutionize the world.

When the Bible says, "No" it gives a reason. When the scripture says, "Do" it has a purpose.

Dr. Luke, medicine man, was detailed, practical, and dealt with the basic rules of living that lead to a spiritual life. What he churned out was a realistic understanding of life where there was substance and fulfillment. The Pharisees missed that understanding of life as they continually made rules. They made those rules as hard and unbending as possible. The rules themselves became the basis of life rather than life being the ruler of rules. Now don't misunderstand me. I am all for rules for the right reason. Without them we would live in chaos and immorality, a "I'll take what you have" mentality that is selfish and egocentric. Rules for life bring ethics, morals, values, and absolutes that are important for us.

Here are some basic rules for living from Jesus today.

First basic rule for living — grace in our poverty and need (Luke 6:20-21a).

Poverty exists around the world and touches every country in the world. Basic human needs like water, food, clean air, living spaces, and more are inadequately provided for millions of people. The poverty in Israel during Jesus time in Israel was real and exploited by the rich. Similarly today people are kept on poverty wages and starvation diets in order for some rich individuals to financially succeed. When Jesus says that the poor are to be blessed he isn't happy about their circumstances. He is saying that through God's grace they too can be a part of the kingdom of God.

I remember hearing about the Phineas Bresee who started the Church of the Nazarene. One of his advertisements in the local newspaper invited everyone to church services where they could sit in the front row. In the late 1800s many of the churches had individuals buy their pew and the closer to the front the more financially powerful one was in the community. Bresee believed that everyone was entitled to a front row seat whether they were rich or poor.

The idea of grace has its roots in the Old Testament that describes the compassionate response of a superior to an inferior, suggesting that the kindness demonstrated was totally underserved. The New Testament broadens the concept of grace by describing it as a difference between human effort to attempt to win God's favor versus receiving God's gift of salvation, which is an expression of his gracious action. Don Campbell wrote, "Grace can be defined therefore as God's unmerited favor in the giving of his Son, through whom salvation is offered to all."

Our spiritual poverty recedes as God gives us his richness. Human poverty may still be real, but spiritual poverty can be replaced. As Christians we are to reach into human poverty and get our hands dirty by helping those in need. This is also true of spiritual poverty. As Christians we are to help others find the richness of God's grace!

Second basic rule for living — hope in our weeping and need (Luke 6:21b).

Where does hope stem from in life?

It stems from help from God. Dr. W.T. Purkiser said that the future belongs to those who belong to God and that this is the foundation of hope.

A Jewish refugee during World War II in Poland wrote, "I believe in the sun even when it isn't shining. I believe in love even when I am alone. I believe in God even when he is silent." (Albert Wells, *Inspiring Quotations*, p.90).

It stems from others helping us along the way. We need the testimony of others who have gone through the same circumstances we are going through. Don't think you are the only one who is facing a unique situation. Others have gone through it and will help you to overcome...if you let them. There is a song with the thought, "Lean on me" when problems arise and needs are overwhelming. Who do you know that you can lean on? These are the people who bring us hope unlimited!

It stems from purpose in life. Hope introduces me to my purpose in life. It was Aristotle who wrote, "It concerns us to know the purposes we seek in life, for then, like archers aiming at a definite mark, we shall be more likely to attain what we want."

What purpose do you have in life? Are you living a Christian life with Christ at the center? Are you living a life of purity and holiness? Is it a life that reaches out to others in their bumps and bruised state? Are you making a difference around the world and locally by caring about situations that really matter?

Endurance through the stretch of life — Neil Orchard wrote about a farmer that he was conversing with concerning his soybean and corn crop. The rains had been abundant and the crops were prize winning. The farmer's comment caught Orchard off guard, "My crops are especially vulnerable. Even a short drought could destroy them."

Orchard then asked him why that would be. The farmer went on to explain that while people often see rains as a benefit, there are times during which the plants are not required to push roots deeper in search of water. The roots, therefore, remain near the surface. A drought would find the plants unprepared and might quickly kill them.

"Some Christians receive abundant 'rains' of worship fellowship and teaching." He continued, "Yet when stress enters their lives, many suddenly abandon God or think him unfaithful. Their roots have never pushed much below the surface. Only roots grown deep into God (Colossians 2:6-7) help us endure times of drought in our lives." (Craig Larson, *Illustrations for Preaching and Teaching*, Grand Rapids: Baker Book House, 1993, p. 65).

Third basic rule for living — acceptance (Luke 6:22-23).

Even if we feel excluded, reviled, and lied about by people for Jesus' sake, God still accepts us.

He knows our hearts. We can tell God anything that's on our hearts, our minds, or our spirits. Gladys Hunt was quoted in *Eternity* magazine in October, 1969. "Acceptance means you are valuable just as you are. It allows you to be the real you. You are not forced into someone else's idea of who you are…You can talk about how you feel inside, why you feel that way, and someone really cares. Acceptance means you can try out your ideas without being shot down. You can express heretical thoughts and discuss them with intelligent questioning." I thought what she said next was very important. "No one will pronounce judgment on you even though they don't agree with you…It simply means it's safe to be you and no one will destroy you out of prejudice." (Charles Swindoll, *The Tale of the Tardy Oxcart*, p.3)

We should feel safe in the church to share our thoughts, ideas, spirits, and more with this safety net under us. If God allows that, don't you think that as the church we should be that accepting?

That doesn't mean we won't be corrected or shown wrong, but it does mean it will be with a sweet spirit and not a harsh Pharisaical spirit!

Let's allow God to help us with the basic rules of living!

Amen.

Epiphany 7
Luke 6:27-36

Revolutionary Rules For Living

Author Bob Welch observed that in *Les Miserables* that the uprising that Victor Hugo observed occurred in June, 1832 as a small Parisian insurrection that lasted only a short time. It was more of a street riot with a tragic outcome. Quoting Hugo, Welch said that the uprising was a defiance against the royalist government of France as a reaction to three problems of the day. First it was a defiance of man by the exploitation of his labor. Second, it was in opposition of the ruination of women by starvation and subservient autocracy and the abomination and cruelty with monstrous abuses against children. The violence that broke out that fateful June was triggered by death, cholera, of a popular liberal politician and former Napoleonic general, Jean Maximilien Lamarque.

Many of the world's revolutions have the same generic principles.

Welch wrote that for many today Jesus has been "relegated to a sort of 'nice guy' and 'cool teacher' status. Actually, he was far edgier than that." Reading the scriptures we get the true sense of who Jesus was as a real revolutionary leader and force of life. Just as he challenged the status quo of his day and he continues to do so in our day.

He granted women status where none existed in their culture. The concept of divorce was rocked when Jesus refused to give *carte-blanche* to the male society who believed in a no-fault divorce for husbands only. He revolutionized the way the world viewed justice individually and nationally. He looked deep into the souls and hearts of humanity and championed the concept that we are redeemable. Jesus' companions were the ordinary people of society.

The ultimate radical idea of Jesus versus the cultural and religious society of the day was that of compassion and love for others.

He calls us to live with the adventurous faith that defies the world. It means follow-the-leader of purity and heart holiness, not the cadence of the culture of leadership of today's society. It is an abandonment of lifeless mundane living to a life of reckless joy that comes as Jesus breaks the forces of evil and sin in our lives!

How does his revolutionary thought coincide with ours? What should we do with his concepts?

Revolutionary principle number 1: Love your enemies (Luke 6:27a).

Ouch! Love my enemies? This is not the emotional sentimental love that the world sometimes describes in a Hallmark movie. Reuben Welch described this as a love that is the active, unlimited spirit of goodwill in the face of opposition and wrong. It genuinely cares for others and wants the best for them...even if it means a transformation of life. Friedrich von Hugel, an influential Austrian Roman Catholic layman, was a Christian apologist writer who died on January 27, 1925. According to Welch, Hugel's last words were, "Christianity taught us to care. Caring is the greatest thing. Caring matters most." (*Beacon Bible Exposition*, page 77).

I struggle with this concept, but the radical Jesus challenges me to look at my enemy in a different light. What is the reason this person is my "enemy"? Have I done something to provoke him/her? Is there something I said that would make me an enemy? What in their background would upset them to think that I am their enemy? How can I win them as a friend or at least a non-threat?

Jesus does not allow me to spit out venom against individuals. We can soften the blows that come our way by expressing God's love toward those people.

"God calls his children to a countercultural lifestyle of forgiveness in a world that demands an eye for an eye — and worse" wrote Brennan Manning.

A word of caution. Jesus did not allow himself to be used as a doormat, nor should we. He stood up to the Pharisees, turned over tables in the temple when he saw the wrong being done to the poor, he used words as a weapon calling the religious leaders "whitewashed tombs" (Matthew 23:27 NIV). Remember he went to the cross for those very people! How far will we go for others?

Revolutionary principle number 2: be a do-gooder! (Luke 6:27b-28).

"Do good" is the principle that revolutionizes culture, society, and individuals. Selfishness, hatred, and evil of every kind seeps through our world. Sin is at the heart of it all. Jesus comes along and says, "Stop sinning. Stop doing evil. Stop the tipsy-topsy world that is no longer balanced and get it right side up…do good!"

Do good by being generous. The late Tom Drake tells that woven into one Christmas Eve, God gave him a crazy mission for Christmas day. He related that it would become the highlight of his year.

Here was the mission. He said that God gave him a plan to stand out on the street corner and hand out $5 bills. Laughingly, he says that this would not be a thought that came on his own because it was not in his nature to be generous, especially to strangers. At first he rejected the idea thinking how bizarre it really was to put into practice, but against his better judgment, he got a piece of cardboard and wrote, "Merry Christmas…Free Money."

He spotted a great place on the corner of a busy intersection. Within moments a car slowed and looked at the sign, but as Tom approached the auto, the man wagged his head and mouthed "no" and sped away. He grumbled to himself, "Whose idea was this, anyway!"

Quickly however, things changed dramatically as a few people rolled their windows down and took the $5 bills he stuffed into their face. He said that traffic increased when his picture got posted on the Facebook page of the local newspaper. Before long he ran out of the $5 bills and he went home. Hours later, frozen and broke, he called it a day.

His take home from all of this? "I discovered giving to others was in exhilarating experience! When we do generous things, something happens deep down in our soul. When we give to others, in a surprising way, you are the one who gets the most out of it…The payoff isn't in the 'thank you' but in the act of giving itself." (Randall Hartman, *Tom's List*, 2016, pp.55-56. Used by permission.)

Can I get personal? When is the last time you "gave something away?" How did you feel? Has it been too long ago to remember? Jesus is ready to revolutionize your life by helping you be generous!

Being good is by serving others. In "Letters to Rulers of People" Francis of Assisi stated it well:

"Keep a clear eye toward life's end. Do not forget your purpose and destiny as God's creature. What you are in his sight is what you are and nothing more.

Remember that when you leave this earth, you can take nothing that you have received…but only what you have given; a full heart enriched by honest service, love, sacrifice, and courage."

That giving is making a difference in another's life.

I believe that the measure of an individual is the fact that he/she serves people.

To the Christian the symbol of service is a lopsided crude, splintery cross with a towel and basis at its base. Who will take them up? Will you?

Revolutionary principle number 3: patience in the midst of opposition (Luke 6:29-36).

Oswald Chambers who wrote *My Utmost for His Highest*, from his lectures at Clapham 1911-1915, and talks at Zeitoun, Egypt in 1915-1917, has many rich thoughts that he shares. One of those thoughts deals with patience.

He writes: "A river is victoriously persistent, it overcomes all barriers. For a while it goes steadily on its course, then it comes to an obstacle and for a while it is blocked, but it soon makes a pathway round the obstacle." Then Chambers zeros in on what this means for the Christian. "You can see God using some lives, but into your life an obstacle has come and you do not seem to be of any use. Keep paying attention to the source, and God will either take you round (it) or remove it...Never get your eyes on the obstacle or on the difficulty, but rather on God!

(Quoted in Jan Karon, *Patches of Godlight*)

Here are some practical thoughts for patience in the midst of opposition.

- In our weakest moments we should turn to the Holy Spirit to give us strength and enduring power (Romans 8:24-30).
- In our obstacles of life put faith into practice and seek God's direction through his word for the right way to persevere (2 Thessalonians 1:4-5).
- Admit our weaknesses and seek opportunities to change direction (Hebrews 11:13-16).
- Choose right and reject the wrong. After all it is your choice! (Psalm 75:2).
- Wait for the right time to act (Habakkuk 2:3).
- Realize that our obstacles build our character and our hope (Romans 5:2-4).
- Gather the saints of God around you to give you strength, courage, understanding, and wisdom (Revelation 6:9-11).

The person who said, "Patience is a bitter plant that produces sweet fruit" was right. Ask God today for the patience you need to overcome the hurts, pain, or obstacle that you are going through today!

Conclusion

If Jesus is a revolutionary, can his followers be anything less?

Amen.

Transfiguration Sunday
Luke 9:28-36 (37-43a)

Rock Stars At The Top

If I were a Hollywood writer, the Transfiguration story would be a great setting. I could see it ranking right up there with "The Ten Commandments," "Samson and Delilah," "The Greatest Story Ever Told," or any of the others. I would title it, "Rock Stars At The Top." The stars would include Jesus, Moses, Elijah, Peter, James, John, and the Voice and I'm still contemplating who I would cast in the roles. It would be a great media-hype type movie with spectacular special effects…a hard to climb mountain, Moses and Elijah suddenly come out of nowhere to be with Jesus who is wearing a halo and an angelic face, clothes that have a razzle dazzle appearance and a glowing Christ. Peter, James, and John are trembling as suddenly Elijah and Moses disappear, a cloud covering them and a voice would come out of the cloud sounding like Morgan Freeman.

If not careful, we are hooked on the supernatural… the spiritual ecstasy of religiosity. We are, as Bruce Larsen observed, "…programmed to expect the big, the unusual, and the spectacular, and we miss the glory of the ordinary."

Focusing on the "Rock Stars At The Top" brings us to the ordinary connections of life. Looking back we think of Moses and Elijah being extraordinary human beings, but they were ordinary people God called to complete a task. They succeeded! What God longs to do is use ordinary people who are willing to obey to make a difference in other people's lives. He will connect his Spirit with those willing individuals every time! On the mountain that night God sent Elijah and Moses to confirm Jesus' ministry.

As the disciples faced the trio they could see Moses who represented the law on one side of Jesus, and Elijah who represented the Prophets on the other side of Christ. The Lord is standing in the middle representing grace.

First, the character of Moses represents God's laws standing on one side of Jesus. He is most famous for carrying down Ten Commandments from Mount Sinai, breaking the tablets into pieces, and then trekking back up the mountain. So we may ask, beside the Ten Commandments what about the "laws" that are included in the Old Testament? As one writer suggested, it encompasses the entire Pentateuch...the first five books of the Old Testament. Contained within these scrolls, laws were set down for physical, dietary, penal, and societal welfare. Many of the laws of the day were cultural and put in place to help the early Hebrews to avoid sickness, suffering, and sanctions and to give guidance and direction for living as a nation and individually. The laws were given to help control the Hebrews' relationship with one another and with him. They culminated in the Ten Commandments. The Hebrew word translated as commandments literally means *words* and gives us a glimpse of the character of God and the revelation of the message he wanted to share with his people. Those of us who are English speaking relate these commandments more as authoritarian, rules and regulations that are unbreakable. They set in motion the moral laws of God to be acted upon and lived. Each generation has had to find in the details what the moral law means for them…how it is lived out. God's laws do not change.

What is the purpose of the law?
- The law helps us become conscious of sin (Romans 3:20).
- The law helps us find Christ so that we might be justified by faith (Galatians 3:24).
- The law helps us by providing protection. Instead of utter chaos in society and on the individual level there is a stability and orderly conduct. People grasp what civility means.
- The law helps us feel secure by giving direction to life.

Laws are like fences. A fence keeps those things we want safe inside and keeps unwanted distractions outside as to not harm us (Joshua 1:8).

Nine of the Ten Commandments, the exception being about the sabbath, are repeated in the New Testament letters. John Witmer wrote, "…church-age believers are to live on a higher level, being empowered by the indwelling Holy Spirit." This is the continual leadership of the Spirit in our lives to act in step with God.

A great question we should ask ourselves is: "Am I displaying God's 'law' by displaying the fruit of the Holy Spirit in my life?

The law defines who we are, who we are to become,

and how we should act toward God, others, and ourselves.

Second, the character of Elijah represents the prophets. Most people see only the area of "foretelling" as the major assignment of the prophets. That was a minor part of the job. The major portion of their assignment was to fit into their day and be the yellow caution light or railroad crossing for the way people ignored or flippantly challenged the living God! They were the visible and vocal conscience for the people of Israel who constantly rebelled, sinned, or hurt God.

It is the prophetic word through the prophets that signaled a new day would dawn when the Messiah would come. He would lead his true followers out of the bondage of Egypt (sin) and create them as the delivered covenant people of God. As Reuben Welch observed, "And to this great new deliverance through the death of Messiah both the law and prophets bear witness."

Third, the character of Jesus represents salvation. The talk on the mountain revolved around his death, but the glory of his resurrection was the promise of the power for eternal life for all who would accept him.

Salvation is God's work as he provided a way for the human race to be delivered from sin's awful grip on our lives. It has come by Christ's sacrificial death on the cross...a conscious decision on God's part (John 3:16). It comes through my faith in Christ. No one else can save me from my sins and no one else can ask for my forgiveness. This Jesus has come to deliver, rescue, preserve, and deliver me from the sin in my life. I like what John Walvoord wrote that looking at the multifaceted doctrine of salvation is like "looking into a ka-

leiduscope of theological terms." Those terms include:
- Grace (Ephesians 1:7, 2 Timothy 1:9)
- Redemption (Romans 3:24, 1 Corinthians 1:30, Hebrews1. 9:12)
- Forgiveness (Ephesians 1:7, Colossians 1:14)
- Justification (Romans 4:25; 5:16)
- Glory or Glorified (Jude 25, Romans 8:30)
- Inheritance (Colossians 1:12, 1 Peter 1:4)
- Peace (Ephesians 2:15-17, Colossians 1:20)

Cyprian was bishop of Carthage and a notable early Christian writer and martyr in 258. He wrote early in his life to a man named Donatus. In his letter he told Donatus that they were living in a bad world. But in this incredibly bad world he had discovered a group of people who had learned the secret of life. He said, "They have found a joy and a wisdom which is a thousand times better than any of the pleasure of our sinful life." Even though these people are despised and persecuted, they are at ease with themselves. They were masters of their own souls and have overcome the world. Cyprian said they were followers of Jesus saved by his holy grace and they are called Christians! He wanted Donatus to know that he had become one of them!

Today God reaches out to you and me and calls us to him. The question is, will we come to him?

Conclusion

The whole Transfiguration event was both a confirmation of Jesus' servant-messiahship and the promise of his coming glory. Alongside that is the confirmation of salvation for anyone who humbles themselves before the living God!

Coming down from the mountain top experience the three disciples and Jesus run smack dab into a desperate father who needs healing for his son. Each of us will run into the everyday routine of life. Like those disciples at the foot of the mountain we will be powerless, helpless, and faithless without Jesus in our midst!

God's love in us is the greatest strength we can have and we must give it to others!

Amen.

www.ingramcontent.com/pod-product-compliance
Lightning Source LLC
Chambersburg PA
CBHW071731090426
42738CB00011B/2460